U.S. Books Abroad: Neglected Ambassadors

Curtis G. Benjamin

Library of Congress
Washington 1984

Publication of this study has been made possible by a generous gift from Leo N. Albert to the Center for the Book in the Library of Congress.

Library of Congress Cataloging in Publication Data

Benjamin, Curtis G., 1901-1983
    U.S. books abroad.

    Bibliography: p.
    1. Book industries and trade—United States. 2. Book industries and trade—Developing countries. 3. Foreign trade promotion—United States. 4. Books and reading—Developing countries. I. Library of Congress. II. Title. III. Title: US books abroad.
Z479.B46 1983   070.5'0973   83-22245
ISBN 0-8444-0442-X

CONTENTS

PREFACE

Books are a unique medium for transmitting ideas and for encouraging reflective and long-lasting mutual understanding. As publishing consultant and retired president of the McGraw-Hill Book Company Curtis G. Benjamin emphasizes in this study prepared for the Center for the Book in the Library of Congress, books are keys to cultural development, catalysts to trade, and unparalleled (but "neglected") ambassadors of American culture. The center is pleased to make Mr. Benjamin's valuable report available to a wide audience.

The "Benjamin report," as it came to be called during discussions, points out the need for a new international outlook on the part of the entire U.S. publishing community. A renewed cooperative approach, which would bring disparate parts of the U.S. book community together in common cause, would help fulfill the immediate educational and economic needs of Third World countries. Such cooperative endeavors will remain equally essential in the decades ahead as the international publishing environment is transformed by global telecommunications networks, cooperative international library agreements, and multinational electronic publishing.

What of the book in this new environment? Or, for that matter, in today's environment, where, as Curtis Benjamin points out, the perception of America by most Third World countries is formed by American television, movies, and music—and not by American books. This serious problem fortunately is receiving increased attention. For example, in "Selling America in the Marketplace of Ideas" in the March 20, 1983, issue of the *New York Times Magazine*, former ambassador Richard N. Gardner asserts that our government's comparative neglect of its overseas book, educational, and cultural programs denies our foreign policy "one of our greatest sources of strength as a nation."

The role of the book in the future, nationally and internationally, is a prime concern of the Center for the Book in the Library of Congress. Established by Act of Congress in 1977, the center works closely with organizations outside the Library of Congress to promote reading and to enhance appreciation of the book and the printed word in the past, present, and future. It is an informal, voluntary organization, funded primarily by private contributions. As a nonpartisan body with no official connection to the publishing community and no official government policy role, the center was the appropriate sponsor for a discussion of a preliminary version of the Benjamin report on April 11, 1983.

Members of the United States Information Agency (USIA) Book and Library Advisory Committee were special guests at the meeting, which took place at the Library of Congress and is described in the June 6, 1983, issue of the *Library of Congress Information Bulletin*. Other participants included members of the advisory committee for the Benjamin report, representatives of the International Division of the Association of American Publishers (AAP), and staff members from the USIA and the Library of Congress.

Participants urged that the Benjamin report, with minor revisions, be published. They also discussed the not-for-profit private-sector organization proposed by Benjamin (Part 10), particularly the respective roles of the private sector and the government in promoting U.S. books abroad. Are the interests of the private sector and the government identical? Different? Compatible? What is the role of the AAP's International Division? Of the USIA itself? These questions remain. There was agreement, however, that the closest cooperation among U.S. publishers, educators, librarians, members of professional societies, government officials, and officers of multinational commercial firms is needed if books are to play their vital role in enlarging an understanding of American culture.

It should be noted, finally, that *U.S. Books Abroad: Neglected Ambassadors* is not a comprehensive document. As the author points out in the introduction, he has been selective in listing organizations and in the regions of the world he has covered.

Movement toward forming the "National Coalition on Books for Developing Countries" proposed in Part 10 of the Benjamin study has begun. A small group of publishers has met to consider establishing an organizing committee and conducting a feasibility study. The Center for the Book is delighted to have served as a catalyst in this effort. Special thanks go to Leo N. Albert for a contribution that has made this publication possible.

John Y. Cole
Executive Director
The Center for the Book

ACKNOWLEDGMENTS

Many people in addition to the members of the ad hoc advisory committee listed in Appendix H were helpful with this study. Some supplied personal knowledge that had never been recorded. Others provided guidance to little-known sources of published information. Still others criticized drafts of parts of the report of which they had expert knowledge. A few volunteered research assistance in areas of their specialization. For their help of one kind or another, the following are hereby and gratefully thanked.

E. E. Booher, former President, McGraw-Hill Book Co. and former Executive Group Vice President, McGraw-Hill, Inc.; Nak Young Choung, Vice President and Director, International Division, Harper & Row, Inc.; J. Adrian Higham, Vice President, John Wiley & Sons; Riici Inagaki, Managing Director, McGraw-Hill Kogakusha, Ltd., Tokyo; G. Stanley Kendrick, President, Prentice-Hall International; John H. Kyle, Director, University of Texas Press; Peter H. Lengemann, Vice President International, Scott, Foresman & Co.; Richard H. Lamb, Director, Books for Asia Program, The Asia Foundation; Rachel M. Mansfield, Vice President and Editorial Director, McGraw-Hill Ryerson, Ltd., Toronto; Anne Mathews, Graduate School of Librarianship and Information Management, University of Denver; Richard D. Moore, former Director, Office of Cultural Centers and Resources, United States Information Agency; John B. Putnam, Consultant, former Executive Director, Association of American University Presses; Carl T. Sandberg, International Sales Manager, Scholastic, Inc.; Joel W. Scarborough, Special Assistant for Development and Public Affairs, The Asia Foundation; Lloyd H. Scheirer, President, McGraw-Hill Ryerson, Ltd., Toronto; Datus C. Smith, Jr., The Asia Society, former President and Chairman, Franklin Book Programs; Geoffrey M. Staines, InterEditions Paris, France; Warren R. Stone, Executive Vice President International, Addison-Wesley Publishing Co.; Jolanda L. von Hagen, President, Springer-Verlag, New York; David J. Walsh, former Group Vice President, Time-Life Books.

PART 1

Introduction:
The Sponsorship, Purpose, Scope, and Method of the Study

Sponsorship. This study was sponsored by the International Committee of the Center for the Book at the Library of Congress. In its planning and execution, liberal assistance was given by members of the International Division of the Association of American Publishers and by several staff officers of the United States Information Agency (USIA). (The latter organization was known for a short period as the U.S. International Communications Agency, or USICA.) An ad hoc advisory committee, selected from the three involved organizations, contributed heavily to the character, the substance, and the conclusions of the report. (See Appendix H.) Thus the experience, knowledge, and judgment of this smaller group are herein expressed as clear consensus on most matters under consideration.

Purpose. The purpose of the study is to provide a document that endeavors to stimulate renewed and wider awareness, first, of the dire need for U.S. books in less developed countries, and, second, of possible ways and means by which this need may be met, at least partially, under present conditions at home and abroad. We feel that a greater national effort is imperative as matters both of societal morality and enlightened self-interest. A number of years ago, Franklin D. Roosevelt aptly said, "Books are bullets in the battle for men's minds." For decades the British have enunciated and supported the principle that "trade follows the book." Both ideas are today as valid as when they were first expressed. Yet both have been neglected, forgotten almost, in the United States in recent years. All our major export-assistance programs have disappeared because each has either fulfilled or failed its mission or has lost adequate financial support. Probably the most important cause of this retrogression has been the lack of a national consensus—or constituency—arguing that greater distribution overseas of U.S. books and other printed materials is very much in the national interest. There has been no substantial action by American leaders either in or out of government, to build a case

1

for the value of books in promoting mutual understanding among various nations and their citizens. Americans generally appear content to leave the field to others, assuming that foreigners will learn about American society, values, and policies in one way or another, without any special concerted effort on the part of the U.S. private sector or the government. The challenge and the question are these: Can a coalition be mobilized, and if so, how should this be attempted? Certainly, the foundation for such an effort has been prepared. For several years a number of knowledgeable individuals and organizations have been discussing the issue, and the United States Information Agency recently proclaimed a new rationale and policy for its Book Program Division that underscore the importance to the national interest of disseminating serious American books abroad. (See Appendix A.) This study takes up the challenge of this new proclamation.

Scope. Although the study is largely directed to less developed countries, it does not deal in equal force with the needs of all such countries. Several of the countries that are officially classified by the United Nations as "developing" are not in such dire need of assistance. Indeed, a few of them are capable of supplying almost all their book needs. They have the necessary economic resources and publishing facilities, but they have failed to give books a proper rating in their scales of national values and financial priorities. Still others have been severely handicapped by war or civil strife. For these reasons the study has attempted to discriminate in a positive way wherever it seemed appropriate to do so. But it must be understood that no attempt was made to define the particular condition and need of each country, or even of each region, that wants and deserves assistance of some kind from the United States. (For further comment on countries classified as "developing," see Appendix B.)

Method. Given the limited time and resources available, the study had to rely largely on inductive methodology. It employed private as well as published records of past experience, and it drew broadly upon personal knowledge of present programs and problems. It synthesized opinions, judgments, and conclusions so as to represent, as closely as possible, the collective thinking of the members of the advisory committee. So the results should be taken more as a "White Paper" than a definitive analytical statement. Still, the study offers much useful background information and knowledgeable guidance for anyone who is interested in its subject. It is hoped that it will help to generate a resurgence of action by many organizations and individuals, both public and private.

As the reader will quickly discover, what follows was written with a wide audience in mind. Hence, it contains much description, exposition, and explanation that will be commonplace—perhaps even boring—to specialists in the areas that it addresses. Accordingly, the specialist is asked to read patiently.

Plainly the advisory committee and its consultant are solely responsible for the views and opinions expressed herein.

PART 2

The Faltering State of U.S. Book Exports

Looking superficially at the available information on export sales of U.S. books, one would conclude, quite naturally, that export selling has flourished in recent years. The Department of Commerce (Bureau of the Census) reports that for the six-year period 1975-81 the compound annual rate of growth was 16.6 percent, and the value in current dollars grew from $263 million to $592 million, or a gain of 125 percent.

Lower export figures, but perhaps more reliable by definition, are those that have been issued annually by the Book Industry Study Group (BISG) over a slightly different six-year period, 1974–80. (In these "Book Industry Trends" reports, 1980 is the latest year for which actual sales figures are given.) Here total export sales values are given as $292 million for 1974 and $510 million for 1980, a still healthful gain of 75 percent. The annual rates of increase in this six-year period ranged from 6 to 14 percent.

Looking at either of the foregoing two sets of lush sales figures, one's first reaction is exultation for the U.S. book industry and for everyone else who is involved in promoting the distribution and use of U.S. books abroad. But when one pauses to consider the deflating effect of price inflation, the sense of elation turns quickly into dejection. For it is a fact that the prices of the kinds of books that make up most of our exports were nearly doubled in either of the periods under consideration. Obviously, this price inflation canceled almost all the reported current-dollar gain in export sales. So "stagflation" has patently been with U.S. book exporters for rather a long time, and there are no signs pointing to improvement in the near future.

Another somber facet must be added to the gloomy picture: export sales, though pushed by steadily increasing numbers of publishers, have trailed domestic sales by a good margin in recent years. This lag has been a sharp reversal of the earlier trend, when the growth of export sales in the 1950s and 1960s far outpaced domestic sales.

5

The whole story of what has happened in recent years can be read quickly from the following tabulations of sales figures from the BISG "Trends" report.

Industry Sales in Current Dollars		
	1974	1980	Increase
Domestic Sales	$3,190,000	$6,220,000	95.0%
Export Sales	292,000	510,000	77.0%
Total Sales	$3,482,000	$6,730,000	93.0%
(Export sales = 8.4% in 1974 and 6.7% in 1980)			

Industry Sales in Units (Copies)		
	1974	1980	Increase
Domestic Sales	1,409,000	1,694,000	20.0%
Export Sales	112,000	113,000	0.8%
Total Sales	1,521,000	1,807,000	18.8%
(Export sales = 7.4% in 1974 and 6.2% in 1980)			

In comparing the ratios between dollar sales and unit sales in the above tabulations, one must keep in mind the fact that U.S. books of the most exportable types experienced the highest rates of price inflation. In 1980 professional and reference books and college texts constituted about 60 percent of the dollar value of all exports, while general (trade) books (both hardbound and paperbacks) accounted for approximately 26 percent. In 1974, the proportions were about 57 and 24 percent respectively. The higher acceleration of prices of the former types accounts for most of the difference between the above sets of dollar figures and unit-sales figures. Anyone who is interested in further details concerning the types and relative amounts of U.S. books that sell abroad will find in Appendix C an interesting analysis that is based on BISG reports on exports for the years 1974 and 1980. For convenience, the given types classification follows that of the statistical reports issued annually by the Association of American Publishers (AAP).

Now, a final depreciatory fact that must be faced squarely: for all their very high, built-in intrinsic values, book exports are really very small potatoes in the commodity-value scale of total U.S. exports. In the past few years, the dollar value of exported books has ranged from 0.23 to 0.26 percent of the total value of all U.S. commodity exports. These miniscule figures probably explain why so few of our leaders in government and industry have shown real and lasting interest in the national importance of the book as an export commodity—an importance that is, certainly, far above its material dollar-trade value.

Although many public figures readily and stoutly attest the great value of books as the country's best ambassadors abroad, this enthusiasm usually is eclipsed by larger and more pressing interests. And, in truth, book publishers, by and large, have themselves to blame for the low position of their product in the real scale of national importance. They have failed to convince the general public of the importance of books in international relations—indeed, all but a handful of them have made no effort whatsoever to do so. They have also failed to agree among themselves on imperative questions of policy relating to government assistance programs. And too often they have been unwilling to accommodate themselves pragmatically to the demands and limitations that are inherent in government-financed support programs. Sad to say, this lack of a concerted spirit of cooperation, connected with a lack of understanding of the imperatives of government operations, appears to be largely responsible for the eventual loss of most of the government support that book exporting enjoyed in the middle years of the century. And even sadder to say, exports to less developed countries have been the hardest hit by the recent losses of that government support. This is, to be sure, a crucial matter to our country at the present precarious moment in international relations. Significantly, other leading nations, both friendly and unfriendly, have lost no time in their efforts to fill the book gaps that we have left open to them. More will be said specifically about this later.

PART 3

The Influence of Multinational Publishing

The rise in multinational operations by several large U.S. publishers has helped to change the pattern and to diminish the level of U.S. book exporting. This development, though it has grown steadily over the past twenty years, has been little noted by the book industry. Perhaps its rise and influence can best be understood in historical perspective.

Before World War II, only a few U.S. publishers had even limited interest in export markets. They were, with one or two exceptions, producers of scientific, technical, and medical books. Most of them had exclusive arrangements with importing agencies in the major export markets, namely, Canada, the United Kingdom, Australia, Japan, and the Philippines. Other foreign markets, all marginal, were left to the three or four active book-exporting firms, each of which represented a good number of U.S. houses. Publishers of general-interest books that had international attraction usually licensed English-language republication rights to U.K. publishers, who customarily acquired thereby exclusive sales rights to all traditional "British Empire" markets—which meant, in effect, all overseas markets where English-language books could be promoted and sold profitably. Such arrangements were fully satisfactory to almost all U.S. trade book publishers; they were preoccupied with their own large and fast-growing home market. Moreover, this kind of arrangement often was quite favorable to the U.S. publisher because it encouraged the idea of reciprocity whenever a U.K. trading partner came to other-way licensing of U.S. rights in an attractive new title. Indeed, the idea of reciprocal trading still dominates the thinking and planning of many trade book publishers on both sides of the Atlantic. It partly accounts for the fact that trade books as a class do not rank higher in the U.S. export scale.

With the advent of World War II, things changed radically. Neither British nor German publishers could maintain their strong positions in international markets. Consequently, most of the world demand for books—and for technical books in particular—shifted to the United States. Naturally, a good number of our publishers rushed in to meet this sudden demand, some boldly, others tentatively. Thus they discovered for the first time how to exploit export markets directly. In doing so, they discovered, also, that exporting required specialized knowledge and much extra effort. They found that marketing and service costs were much higher, and that risks were far greater. Further, a much higher ratio of working capital to sales-volume was required to finance dispersed inventory and longterm receivables. (The latter was 180 days or longer for export accounts, a painful contrast with the customary 60 days for domestic accounts.) Also, most American publishers had to learn, often painfully, how to deal with the "funny-money" currencies of the world. Somehow, a higher profit margin had to be attained—a problem for which a generally satisfactory solution has yet to be found.

During the war years and those immediately following, most of the larger U.S. publishers opened branch offices abroad. They were located, usually, for sales promotion and distribution services on a regional pattern. The specialized publishers of scientific, technical, and medical books again led the way. Their books had built-in appeal for worldwide recognition of American leadership in educational methodology and in scientific and industrial development.

Most of these overseas branch offices flourished in size and in their own resources. With this prosperity came the urge to start indigenous publishing on their own. It was a temptation that could not be denied by the more venturesome. So a few U.S. firms became international publishers as early as thirty or forty years ago. In time, the idea caught on more widely. By mid-century a fairly large number of American publishers, observing earlier successes, had become internationally minded, and their export sales had increased tenfold over prewar levels.

Then, in the 1960s and the 1970s, came the rapid development of what was truly "multinational" publishing by the larger U.S. houses. Many of their foreign branch offices were turned into subsidiary corporations—some wholly owned, others partly owned, depending usually on the law of the country of domicile. Some of these "offshore" corporations became important, even dominant, publishers for the local area while continuing to serve as sales outlets for their parent companies. In addition to indigenous titles, their lists included translated or adapted English-language editions; and in some instances they also produced paperback reprints of their parent-company's textbooks and

10

professional books.

The multinational pattern of overseas expansion led, inevitably, to acquisitions of foreign companies, many of which continued to operate under their own imprints as parts of what were, organizationally, international "conglomerates."

Through the two kinds of multinational growth processes, several very large American publishers have become all but denationalized. Each of them has, in effect, several home markets and many export markets. In a sense, all their markets are "overseas," which means that each of the subsidiaries sells the books of all their "sister" publishing subsidiaries as well as those of the parent company. Thus many former importing branch offices have become in themselves sizable exporting subsidiaries. And thus a few large firms have created publishing and sales networks that cover most of the civilized world.

By studying the 1982 edition of Bowker's *Literary Market Place* (LMP), one finds that in that year thirty-two U.S. publishers reported ownership of eighty-two foreign subsidiaries. Eight firms listed five or more, and three listed ten or more. The largest of these had fourteen—ten wholly owned, four partly owned. Indigenous English books were published by six of the fourteen subsidiaries; the other eight published only in foreign national languages or regional dialects. Of the other larger multinational firms, each with from five to ten subsidiaries, most published indigenous English-language titles only in Canada, the United Kingdom, or Australia.

As to the location of the eighty-two subsidiary companies, the most favored countries were, of course, the same three: Canada with twenty, the United Kingdom with fifteen, and Australia with eight. These leaders were followed by Japan with six, then by India, Mexico, and Brazil with four each. New Zealand, France, and the Philippines had three each.

Given the rapid increase in the number and size of offshore publishing subsidiaries, accompanied by "incestuous" trading among them, it was inevitable that much of the supply of books to foreign markets would shift away from the U.S. parent companies. For example, the largest of the multinational firms (the one noted above) reported that in 1981 approximately 61 percent of all its books sold in foreign markets were published abroad. (In 1974 the proportion had been 55 percent; ten years earlier it probably was no more than 15 percent.) Another large multinational publisher stated its 1981 offshore production at 50 percent, while still others reported from 20 to 30 percent.

11

Further, with the growth of multinational publishing, many U.S. firms have reported substantial increases in the "foreign" portion of their total annual income—"foreign" meaning, in this case, all offshore sales, properly adjusted for intercompany transfer of unsold goods. For 1981, several firms reported such sales as contributing as much as 20 to 30 percent of their total gross income—this while the book industry average was, as we have seen, no higher than 7 to 8 percent.

The various regional patterns for organizing multinational sales and distributive services follow similar lines. The Canadian company usually serves all provinces, but occasionally there is a separate subsidiary company for service to French-speaking markets in the eastern provinces. The U.K. company usually serves the British Isles and Europe (including the Soviet-bloc countries), plus Africa and the Middle East. The Mexican company often serves all of Spanish-speaking Latin America, but in some instances a second, more centrally located subsidiary serves all countries south of Panama. Brazil, also, is sometimes served by a separate company. The Australian company usually serves New Zealand, and often it serves Southeastern Asian countries as well. The Japanese company serves all of Eastern Asia, but in some instances it serves only Korea and Taiwan, leaving Southeast Asia for a Hong Kong, Singapore, or Manila subsidiary. The Indian company usually is hard pressed to serve its own large and complex market, but it often also serves the adjacent smaller national markets of that subcontinent. The People's Republic of China has recently given promise of opening a new area market that could keep book exporters of a dozen nations scrambling for years to establish favorably located trading beachheads. Indeed, China seems to be the last regional frontier of international commerce on planet Earth.

At this point some readers have probably begun to wonder why they have been given such a long account of the development of multinational publishing. Just what has all this to do with exporting U.S. books to less developed countries? The answers to this question are really quite simple. Yet, as noted at the outset, they have hardly been noticed, much less explicated, either by publishers themselves or by outside observers and analysts.

First, the large increase in offshore publishing of English-language titles has taken a substantial competitive toll of the direct-export sales of U.S. titles. In thousands of instances, U.S. books (and textbooks in particular) have been replaced by books published by U.S. subsidiary companies in Canada, or the U.K., or Australia. This preferential replacement has occurred on a large scale, not only in the home markets of overseas subsidiary publishing companies but in the markets of other Commonwealth countries and in those of many former British Empire countries as well. No one knows, or ever will know, how much this self-competition factor has diminished U.S. direct-export sales, but anyone who is familiar with the worldwide picture knows that the loss is substantial.

Second, a more subtle diminishing force has occurred in the area of costs and prices. Increased intramural competition has often caused decreased sales of U.S. books, especially of high-level textbooks, monographs, and professional treatises. Decreased sales have caused smaller printings, and smaller printings have resulted in higher unit costs and prices. High prices have always been the bane of U.S. books in developing-country markets, and this deterrent has become increasingly restrictive in recent years. More will be said later about the omnipresent problem of high prices generally.

Third, necessary but disliked mark-ups of U.S. list (catalog) prices by foreign subsidiaries have added to buying resistance in most overseas markets. Again, this is a subtle, psychological matter. Somehow, many booksellers and most book-buyers seem to think that they should pay no more than the U.S. list price for a book, no matter where the publisher's source of supply is located, be it New York or London or Tokyo or Singapore. Naturally, they do not look upon a subsidiary company as being a regional importer—as a middleman, actually, who must extract a fee for his services. Yet, as noted at the outset, higher margins are necessary to cover the higher costs and risks of exporting, and a mark-up seems to be the only way that this can be done. It is hard to say just how much this psychological factor has penalized the sale of U.S. books in less developed countries, but certainly it has cost a good amount of goodwill, if nothing else.

Fourth, the wide deployment of regional sales and shipping services has made it impossible for book-industry statisticians or the U.S. Department of Commerce or any other interested observer to report anything but a scrambled and misleading geographical account of U.S. book exports. To illustrate the point: Company A requires all importers, retailers, and individual buyers in the Middle East and Africa to order its books from its London-based subsidiary, but all sales to those two less developed areas are recorded by the parent company as sales to the U.K., for that is where the books were shipped originally. The same is true of orders shipped to other European countries by the U.K. subsidiary. Obviously, the same kind of situation and result occurs when Company B's Singapore subsidiary serves all Southeast Asian countries, or when Company C's Mexican or Panamanian subsidiary serves all South American countries. Naturally, this kind of multinational regional distribution induces gross overstatements of imports by the countries where subsidiaries are customarily based, and equally gross understatements of purchase by the countries that are served by the subsidiaries. Some publishers consider this distortion of export sales statistics to be a trivial matter. Nevertheless, it does seriously mislead uninformed observers as to the true market potentials of many countries, and those of smaller, less developed countries in particular. Also, the distortion can harmfully misguide efforts to organize assistance programs for needy countries on an even-handed basis—a matter that lies at the heart of this study.

The reader who may be inclined to discount what has here been said about the recently burgeoning impact of multinational publishing should cogitate the fact that the largest ten of our multinational firms account for as much as 70 to 80 percent of the total "foreign" sales of U.S. book publishers. Yes, this new wave is indeed high and powerful, and it is propitious to much of our industry. Still, it has had certain subtle erosive effects that are not altogether welcome.

PART 4

The Impact of English-Language Publishing in Continental Europe

Here we should note another significant change in foreign publishing that has helped to depress U.S. book exports in recent years. This is the advent of original publishing in English by many of the larger Continental European publishers, and by those of Germany, of Holland, and of the Scandinavian countries, in particular. Like the rise of the effect of multinational publishing, this practice came gradually as a sea change that has been almost unnoticed by U.S. book publishers generally. Perhaps this is because the practice has arisen almost exclusively among publishers of scientific and technical books—areas of publishing that neither seek nor attract much attention by the news media on either side of the Atlantic.

The practice started in 1964 when Springer Verlag (by far the largest technical publisher in West Germany, possibly the largest in the world) experimented with dual editions of certain high-level titles, the one in German for the "home" market, the other in English for export markets. They soon found that the English edition often outsold the German edition by two or three to one. Later, they discovered that an English edition would sell about as well as the German and English edition combined. Most buyers of their books, it seemed, could read each language with equal ease. (In fact, many university students preferred to buy the English edition—they could at the same time learn the subject matter and perfect their knowledge of English, the lingua franca of their academic world.) Thus, the leading German firm became in time a publisher primarily of English-language books. In 1982, Springer Verlag, GmbH, produced over eight hundred titles, of which 56 percent were published in the English language only, and 6 percent in dual editions.

Of course, other large German technical houses were not slow to catch on. Their progress in doing likewise cannot be exactly measured, because Börsenverein des Deutschen Buchhandels E.V. does not publish the relevant statistics. But a knowledgeable observer estimates that the seven leading German technical publishers currently produce between 800 and 900 English-language titles per year. Further, this observer estimates that the seven "biggies" account for about 70 percent of the total annual D.M. value of West German book exports. Also, that between 70 and 80 percent of their English-language publications are exported.

Concurrently, several Dutch publishers followed suit briskly and successfully. With very limited markets for their Nederlander books, some of them were soon into English-language publishing even more heavily than were the Germans. Their two very large technical houses, the Elsevier/North Holland Group and the Kluwer N.V. Group, now publish about 70 percent of their annual lists in English-language editions only. And our expert European observer estimates that the two houses alone currently account for at least 60 percent of Holland's total annual volume of book exports.

Moreover, several Swedish publishers have to be reckoned with in this matter for they were closely on the heels of the Germans. The largest two of their technical book publishers, Tannum and Munskgaard, each now produces a good portion of its annual list in English-language editions only—about 25 percent for the former and 40 percent for the latter. And here again most of the English-language product is exported worldwide.

In summary, it is amply evident that several large publishing houses in West Germany, Holland, and Sweden have emerged as important producers of English-language books of high quality and highly exportable character. When their large output is added to the smaller outputs of such countries as Norway, Denmark, Finland, Austria, Yugoslavia, Czechoslovakia, and Switzerland (plus Japan, Singapore, and India), it can readily be seen that U.S. book exporters have met with a new kind of formidable competition. But here again it must be conceded that neither the force nor the result of this new competition can possibly be measured. Yet it has been a patently significant factor in diminishing the dominant position of U.S. books in many developing countries of the world. And no doubt it had much to do with the fact that the exported proportion of West Germany's annual book sales jumped from 13 percent in 1970 to 30 percent in 1972, then to 50 percent in 1982.

PART 5

Major U.S. Assistance
Programs of the Past

The following descriptions of a few of the larger and more effective government-aid programs of past years are offered with three purposes in mind: first, to inform younger members of our book-interested communities; second, to refresh the memories of older members about details that may have faded a bit murkily; and, third, to state or imply the strong and weak characteristics of each program, so that something of current value may be learned, perhaps, from hard experiences of the past.

The Informational Guaranty Program (IMG). This was a program whereby producers of U.S. books, magazines, films, musical recordings, and other informational media were able to sell their materials in countries that were short of hard-currency foreign exchange. Local "soft" currencies were accepted, and convertibility into U.S. dollars was guaranteed, first by the European Recovery Program of 1948, then by the Mutual Security Acts of 1951 and 1952. The International Information Agency (IIA) in the Department of State ran the program until 1953, when it was turned over to the newly created United States Information Agency (USIA), which managed it for the next sixteen years.

The IMG Program was established solely to help overcome foreign exchange barriers. Although its implicit relationship to the government's economic and technical assistance efforts and its obvious contribution to the stimulation of foreign trade were important, its basic purpose as stated by the Congress was to serve as an adjunct to the government's international information activities. Thus its location in the Department of State was certainly logical. Had its main purpose been trade stimulation or technical assistance, it would properly have been located elsewhere, perhaps in the Department of Commerce.

The legislative language of the Mutual Security Act of 1951 specified that eligible information "media" were deemed to include books and other materials that "must reflect the best elements of American life and shall not be such as to bring discredit

17

upon the United States." Ineligible publications were those that were patently lewd or salacious, or those that contained "political propaganda inimical to the best interests of the United States," or those that were of very specialized or "trivial" interest. Thus, from the very first year, problems of opinionated selection and censorship were inherent and persistent. Protests from U.S. producers and foreign purchaser were increasingly heard. Finally, in 1961, the USIA issued a list of specific materials that qualified for the program. This list excluded all commercial motion pictures, plus several other classes of works that had only entertainment value. Naturally, movie producers and publishers of belle-lettristic books were resentful of these exclusions, and so were publishers of works of non-American background. Predictably, the cries of "censorship" were intensified. The American Book Publishers Council sent a strong letter of protest to the USIA, but it was preemptively rejected. To many, this seemed to be strange indeed for a government that had always strongly embraced the tenet that responsible criticism is a hallmark of democracy.

Officially, IMG operation began with a bilateral diplomatic agreement between the U.S. government and that of the participating country. Based on this arrangement, USIA made guaranties to all U.S. exporters whose proposals to make sales in the participating countries had the government's approval.

The guaranties were contracts between USIA and the exporter. The contracts established the level of USIA's liability to the exporter, the time limits of the guaranty, the types of materials covered by the guaranty, and so forth. Thereafter, the exporter pursued his business with importers in the participating country in a normal fashion, protected only against the hazard of accepting blocked currency in payment for sales. Upon receipts of payment in such currency, the exporter applied to the agency for conversion and presented his draft for U.S. currency. The agency then caused the exporter to receive from the Treasury a dollar check equivalent in value to the nonconvertible foreign currency proceeds of the sale, and the Treasury deposited the foreign currencies to an account where they were available for use (in exchange for appropriated dollars) by the U.S. government in the participating country. The appropriated dollars received by USIA in exchange for foreign currencies were deposited in a special account and were available to underwrite additional guaranties. IMG eventually operated in this complicated manner in twenty-one countries. A list of them, together with a time span of operation in each, and amounts of funds contracted and actually spent in each, is given in Appendix D.

Technically, IMG was funded by public debt financing as opposed to annual appropriations. Since the publishers paid a fee of 1½ percent to participate in the program, and since, as noted, the purpose of the program was mere currency convertibility, the program theoretically should have been self-sustaining. The Treasury Department, however, took substantial losses on subsequent sales of depreciated foreign currencies and charged the "differences" to USIA. At the program's termination, the agency had borrowed from the Treasury (or assumed the indebtedness) of $31,620,170. It had paid back $9,509,170 (provided by Congress in appropriated funds), leaving a net borrowing of $22,114,000 still on the Treasury books.

Payments to the publishers in nineteen years of operation were $83,325,033. The agency's debt to the Treasury of $22,114,000, plus the appropriated $9,509,170, indicates that it cost the taxpayer 38 cents for each dollar the publisher received, exclusive of administrative expenses from the agency's budget. This led to charges of "subsidy" by congressional opponents of the program. Although only normal profits accrued to the publisher, the fact that the U.S. government incurred "bookkeeping" losses for private business transactions could logically, if not legally, be considered a cash subvention.

Another constant problem related to finance was the use of the acquired currency. Some needy countries felt that without restrictions on the use of the funds, they were gaining no material advantage in their balance of payments. For example, if they lost the dollar payments for local expenses of the U.S. diplomatic missions and activities, and received instead the IMG converted local currency, the U.S. government was in effect paying expenses in merchandise—i.e., books instead of dollars. Many observers saw the justification for restrictions placed on the use of the currency by the foreign government, but strong congressional objection to a foreign country's ability to veto the free use of funds caused the agency finally to refrain from entering agreements where currency use was restricted. This prevented several countries that were foreign-policy "targets" from entering into IMG agreements.

In the end, the sharply conflicting views brought about the termination of IMG. The eligibility standards continued to be considered too liberal by some and too restrictive by others. To some it was a government propaganda device, to others it was a subsidy of commercial exporters, and to still others it spelled detested censorship. To some the funding method seemed the only feasible way to relate government funding to normal business operations, but to many congressmen it appeared to be "back-door" financing that evaded the original enabling legislation.

The method of financing finally precipitated the termination of the program in 1968. The Senate Appropriations Committee had long voiced its displeasure that the agency was able to secure funds from the Treasury without regular congressional appropriations. So IMG was terminated, not by rescinding its statutory authority but by cutting off funds for its administration. In the agency's appropriation of FY 1967–68, the USIA was expressly prohibited from using any of its funds for salaries or any other operating expense of the program—an easy and simple method of legislated strangulation.

The IMG Program is now only an ambivalent memory to the dwindling number of people around the world who were involved in it. Yet its modus vivendi remains very attractive as a way to overcome what is still one of the biggest obstacles to exporting books to almost all less developed countries. So, no matter how the pros and cons may stack up retrospectively, it seems clear that IMG was successful in several important respects.

—It set a pattern for government and private-enterprise cooperation that did not undercut the regular flow of commerce. Nor did it line the pockets of either exporters or importers.

—It made available millions of copies of U.S. books to needy countries that otherwise would have had to go without in very critical times.

—It taught many American publishers the difficulties and imperatives of dealing with governmental political and regulatory requirements. Hard lessons were learned on both sides.

—It put to good use many millions of excess U.S. counterpart funds that were blocked and deteriorating rapidly in value. (Such funds still moulder today in several Third World countries, and in large amounts in India, Pakistan, and Burma, in particular.)

—It provided a comparatively cheap means for subsidizing overseas distribution of high-grade propaganda materials in support of the goodwill and foreign-policy objectives of our government.

Remembering the facts of IMG operations, a good many aging publishers and a few "old hands" in Washington remain hopeful that a new (and much simplified) IMG-type program will somehow and soon be organized to meet the challenges that are today as critical as they were in the two decades following World War II.

USIA Donated Books Programs. This book program, primarily of the 1960s, consisted of two elements: a people-to-people effort among private organizations, to fill the "book gap" abroad in part with used books, guided and supported by USIA; and a program of assembling and distributing publisher overstocks, remainders, and printing add-ons through USIA's own offices. In the private group activity, USIA soon began to have questions about its involvement in the distribution of unknown books in unknown condition to, in some cases, unknown recipients. Resolving those problems was not possible without considerable added cost to the agency. In the mid-1960s, this book distribution was disengaged from other USIA activities, with the private groups urged to handle the entire process through the private sector, including shipping costs and delivery. USIA support since, except in a few special situations, has been advisory and facilitative.

A quantitatively larger donated-book activity of USIA was the acceptance of excess books from publishers and their distribution to Third World countries designated by publishers as not currently profitable markets. For USIA, this activity yielded several million books per year that were in good physical condition. In addition, annotations of content were available from publisher catalogs. Last, it was possible to deal with multiple copies of single titles. The success of the program in the 1960s was possible, however, largely because of an Internal Revenue Service ruling that allowed publishers a tax deduction of the "fair market value" of their donations. Most publishers, not surprisingly, were quick to take "market-value" as the retail price of a book, and USIA had almost more books than it could ship. But in a 1969 ruling, IRS defined the "fair value" of a donated book as the manufacturing cost. The donations soon plummeted as publishers found more economic means of handling spare books; and by 1982, USIA was receiving only 100,000 books per year. Since 1981, USIA has been studying ways of restoring incentives for such donations, but without success thus far.

USIA Low-Priced Books in Translation (1956-60). In 1956, USIA presented to Congress a low-priced paperback book program and received an immediate favorable response to it. The premise was that what was then beginning in U.S. publishing was

21

applicable elsewhere, and that paperbacks in large editions would sell at very low retail prices to mass audiences. Japanese, Chinese, seven or eight languages in India, Thai, Urdu, Arabic, Greek, and Turkish were the principal languages chosen to launch the program. To further emphasize the commercial nature of the program, USIA subsidized these editions through a U.S. commercial house.

Several problems beset the program: there were insufficient book outlets for the books produced; the low retail prices did not give the booksellers a sufficiently attractive mark-up; there were questions as to how many books were actually printed, since the U.S. company could supervise only infrequently on the scene; and an overly high subsidy gave publishers little incentive to sell. In 1960, this program was terminated in favor of programs supervised by USIA officers who dealt directly, but not always expertly, with the foreign publishers.

USIA Low-Priced Books in English. The 1956 low-priced book program concept also produced a program of full-length American books in English—"Student Editions"—reprinted by American paperback houses in the United States and sold through commercial export channels at low wholesale and retail prices. Located closer to home, the Student Editions program was able to respond more quickly to the problems that caused the translation program to falter. Retail prices gradually rose from 10 cents to 25 cents; print runs were reduced from 50,000 to 25,000 and on more serious titles 20,000 and 15,000—all to adjust printings to the demand through established international book channels. In many ways these editions were ahead of their time, the audience for which books in English are now in demand having only developed slowly over two decades of attention to education and literacy abroad. In any event, other demands on USIA funds led to termination of the Student Editions in 1964.

Ladder Books in Low-Priced Editions. More timely in 1957 was the Ladder Series—paperback editions of American books abridged and adapted in controlled vocabularies for readers of English as a second or foreign language. Publication and distribution practices were the same as for the Student Editions, except the Ladder Edition had the advantage of being salable everywhere in the Third World, rather than only in countries like India where audiences were well educated in English. When initiated in 1957, the series was intended to provide readers with useful books on American culture at a level that the modestly advanced English student could understand. But their linguistic structure led to their adoption first as collateral reading and then as texts for English courses. Probably it was the most successful series that USIA had produced; approximately 70 percent of more than nine million books published were sold. Despite increasing expenses, sales receipts and marketing experience enabled USIA to produce the books at 19 cents per book in 1975, compared to 25 cents in 1957. Limitations on budget, not a decline in usefulness, resulted in termination by USIA of its subsidy in 1975. In Korea and Japan, fortunately, Ladder books were sufficiently profitable to make possible reprints by publishers in those countries without USIA financing. Similar situations may be arising in North Africa and Southeast Asia. Such editions do help somewhat to meet the worldwide demand for English teaching materials, and Ladder books do continue to exist in some areas.

USIA French for Africa Program. The return of DeGaulle to power in France at the beginning of the 1960s led to the rapid transition of Francophone Africa from colonies to countries. Belgium also reacted to the trend of the times by granting independence to the Congo. Faced with new communication problems, USIA responded by creating a French for Africa Book Program in 1962. The African Regional Service Center was created in Paris, and 800,000 copies of translated U.S. books were produced in the first full year of 1963. It was soon found, however, that no commercial system existed for distribution of the books to potential markets in Africa.

This lack led the USIA to an expenditure of some $400,000 more per year to create one. It funded the cost of a Paris office and a staff of five salesmen for a large American exporter. But that arrangement did not work out satisfactorily for either side, so it was terminated in 1967, and the USIA undertook a new, less expensive venture.

Since so much expense went into creating the initial distribution network, no additional funding was available for publishing. Production in Paris began to decrease, from the first year's high of 800,000 to 748,000 copies in 1964, to 781,000 in 1965, and to 640,000 in 1966. By 1967 production was at 531,000 copies, and a new distribution system was developed by a joint arrangement between another U.S. exporter and a large French publisher. But by 1979 production was at 67,000 copies, and financial support for distribution was at zero.

If the 1950s were a period of experimentation, the 1960s produced considerably expanded USIA book programs. One-country language programs that had grown out of the 1956 low-priced translated book programs were producing books in Korean, Chinese, Burmese, Thai, Malay, and soon, if not in large quantities, then at levels that gave U.S. books a respectable presence in bookstores of the countries where these languages were read. In each case, the USIA post in the country now had full responsibility for its programs. The Chinese program eventually developed a "back list" of American studies that continue to be reprinted in thirteenth and fourteenth editions.

But the most active translation program of the early 1960s was a direct result of President Kennedy's "Alliance for Progress" in Latin America. Regional Book Offices were established by USIA in Mexico, Argentina, and Brazil, and AID set up its own offices in those cities to produce scientific and technical books. Figures are not readily available on the AID program, although it is known that perhaps two million books and pamphlets were produced annually in the best years of the ten-year duration of the program. USIA's program produced one million books per year minimum in 1963 in both Spanish and Portuguese and reached a peak of two million in each language in 1966. From there, production began to be contracted under the same budget structures as other USIA programs. In 1982, the two book offices that remained in Mexico and Argentina produced some 300,000 copies. Those offices now primarily identify and promote American books in Spanish published without USIA assistance.

Franklin Book Programs, Inc. This not-for-profit, private-sector organization was started in 1952 under the direction of a board of directors composed of prominent educators, public officials, corporate executives, librarians, and publishers. Though it was not publicly announced at the time, it was organized at the instigation of the International Information Agency (IIA) in the State Department, which saw the need for a nongovernmental, noncommercial agency to provide professional guidance and contractual management of its projected overseas publishing ventures. In fact, the IIA (which a year later became the USIA) wholly financed Franklin's start-up costs through advance contractual arrangements. A few years later, after Franklin had become largely self-supporting and had gained favorable recognition worldwide, the initial government connection was "surfaced" to the credit of the original IIA initiative. Thereafter most of Franklin's operating costs were financed by its own earnings and by contributions from U.S. foundations, corporations, and interested private individuals.

Franklin's program objectives were: "(1) To increase local capabilities through technical assistance and training in the planning, production, and dissemination of educational materials at all levels of developing societies; (2) To increase international exchange of knowledge through translation and copyright services, stimulation of international trade, conferences, and exhibits; (3) To strengthen marketing and distribution of locally produced and imported educational materials; (4) To develop the reading habit through reading-reinforcement materials; library development and utilization particularly for children; assistance to literary campaigns."

Starting initially at Cairo, and operating largely with the start-up funds provided by USIA, Franklin assisted in the production of more than four hundred translated Arabic editions of U.S. books within its first ten years. It acquired translation rights from U.S. publishers for nominal fees, financed high quality translations, and then assigned translated titles to competent local publishers who produced the books on a commercial basis, with a reimbursing royalty paid to Franklin in local currency. This pattern of operations was soon extended to other countries, and within the initial decade some seven hundred other translated editions were published in the Farsi, Urdu, Bengali, Malay, Indonesian, and Pushtu languages.

From these starting programs, Franklin branched out by financing and overseeing the production of new, modern encyclopedias in the Arabic, Farsi, Bengali, Urdu, and Indonesian languages. In addition, it assisted in the indigenous production of textbooks, school magazines, audiovisual materials, technical pamphlets, and higher-level professional books and journals. In later years, the planning and administration of local training programs became a major activity, sponsored usually by developing country governments, especially those included in a Latin America country-to-country program that was started (but underfinanced) in 1976.

In its quarter century of operations, more than three thousand titles were translated and produced through Franklin. For all its programs, more than $100 million was expended in various currencies. About $20 million of this came from U.S. sources, and only $600,000 was contributed in cash by the U.S. book industry. The rest came from earned income and government contracts in foreign countries. (Actually, the U.S. book industry had an even cash balance with Franklin; our publishers received a total of about $600,000 in rights and royalty payments.)

In spite of this outstanding record of success, Franklin Book Programs had to struggle for existence in the 1970s. Anyone who is not thoroughly familiar with Franklin's history might well ask how this could happen. There are several reasons why it did happen, some of them sound, others false or factitious.

First, Franklin fulfilled its original mission in several countries by producing as many translated editions as national or area markets could absorb.

Second, there were, inevitably, a few cases of incompetent, even dishonest, management of field offices. Naturally, they caused a considerable amount of both local and home-office disaffection.

Third, in Iran and Afghanistan, Franklin's activity assisted government-directed monopolies of textbook production, including the design and operation of three new and modern printing plants. This blocked private-enterprise publishing, which disquieted a good number of U.S. publishers who had supported Franklin's efforts in other countries.

Fourth, Franklin forfeited much of its U.S. government support by refusing to limit its sponsorship to books that were strictly in line with U.S. foreign policy objectives as interpreted by USIA program officers. Hassling over this point of principle went on for many years. It was, in fact, a sad repetition of the IMG conflict.

Now, on balance, what can be said of Franklin's overall performance? Well, those who saw both the rise and fall of Franklin's fortune know that Franklin well served the interests of our book industry and our government; and that it served even better the interests of many book-hungry countries around the world, where its model still enjoys much confidence and high reputation.

Although the Franklin Book Program was formally liquidated in 1979, that was not the end of its good influence. Aside from the millions of books published with Franklin's help, there exist, even today, other residual benefits. The most important are, of course, the hundreds of Asians, Africans, and Latin Americans who were trained in the various aspects of book work. Another great contribution was the evolvement of new concepts and methods of cooperating with people in developing countries and offering them technical assistance in ways that were acceptable to them as self-respecting men and women. So the Franklin experience should be kept freshly in mind. Its spirit and its basic ideas can be revived usefully for other programs for other needy countries at later times. And here at home we can still benefit from its valuable lessons of success and failure in organizing work between private enterprise and government agencies.

The Philippines: U.S. Textbook Production Project (TPP). This project, which ran from 1961 through 1966, was probably the largest ever undertaken by the U.S. Agency for International Development (USAID). It was planned to provide for approximately 80 percent of the basic book needs for public elementary and high schools. USAID provided manufacturing materials, technical assistance (notably printing skills and supervision), and down-time use of the USIA regional printing plant in Manila. It also trained locally employed authors and instructional-materials specialists. The Philippine government directed the preparation and selection of the textbooks, contracted with private printers, and was responsible for the distribution of the books.

The overall U.S. dollar contribution to the project was $4.4 million; the Philippine contribution was 65 million pesos ($16.75 million), including some counterpart funds generated by U.S. agricultural aid. In six years, the project produced nearly 25 million textbooks for grades 1-12. Approximately half of the eighty-seven titles produced were specifically written for the project; the remainder were adapted reprints of U.S. titles. Most of the books were extensively illustrated in four colors, casebound with cloth covers, and meant to last a minimum of five years.

About 65 percent of the books were produced by the private Philippine printing industry; thus the project had a major impact on upgrading and providing needed work for that industry. By the end of 1966, the Philippine government was facing an acute economic crisis, and the Department of Education ran out of funds for needed revisions, reprintings, and replacements. So the whole project had to be terminated.

Clearly, the project was managed primarily by printers, and good ones. However, it is not clear whether manuscripts were ever tested in classrooms before production, or whether teacher training was part of the project. In fact, it appears that no one ever investigated how effective the books were in classroom use.

In 1975, when the results of TPP were briefly investigated in the context of appraising a new textbook project for the World Bank, no one was able to locate a single complete set of the texts or to determine what titles had ever been reprinted, revised, or supplemented. By that year, Philippine classrooms once again lacked textbooks to a paralyzing extent.

Third Education Project for Indonesia. This was another inter-governmental project that can be described as a sad echo of the foundered USAID Philippine textbook project. It was planned and approved in 1973 for initial financing by a line of credit with the International Development Association (IDA) amounting to U.S. $13.5 million. (The IDA is an arm of the World Bank that makes long-term "credit loans" to very poor countries only; its resources and operating methods are far too complex to permit description here.) The total cost of the Indonesian Project was estimated in 1973 to be $40 million, but by November 1978 the amount had increased to $105 million, of which the greater part by far was paid by the Indonesian government. Other agencies involved in the original IDA credit-loan were the government of Canada (largely paper supplies), UNICEF, and the World Bank.

The enormous project had three primary purposes: (1) the provision of elementary and secondary level textbooks of American origin; (2) improvements in teacher's education and classroom skills; (3) strengthening of the primary school inspectorate. It would also encourage and coordinate curriculum development as the writing and production of the new textbooks progressed. From inception, it suffered from a lack of focus on institution-building, on the development of professional publishing capabilities, and on the training and retention of adequate staff. Little attention was paid to manuscript development, and the project experienced continuous problems with the testing, production, and distribution of its products.

In spite of these failures, the project did produce more than 100 million books before its conclusion at the end of the 1978–79 budget year, making it one of the largest textbook projects ever undertaken. Unfortunately, delays of up to two years in production schedules caused by slow financial and publishing procedures (and no doubt unrealistic schedules) caused considerable dislocation in the concurrent training program for teachers. Nor were books ever delivered to schools on time for the beginning of the academic year. As with the Philippine project, considerably more time and effort were spent on physically producing books and on the taxing problems of distribution than on ensuring that the texts were suitable for classroom use and would be properly used. Further, the project accomplished little toward developing publishing competence and toward building an indigenous publishing industry.

Joint Indo-American Textbook Program. There is general consensus among Indian and American educators, government officials, publishers, and other informed observers that Indian higher education was well served by a major and generous U.S. government-subsidy textbook reprint program carried on in India during the decades of the 1960s and the 1970s.

Using surplus Indian rupee funds generated through the sale of U.S. grain to the government of India during the 1950s, the USIA launched in New Delhi a textbook-subsidy reprint program in the early 1960s. The Joint Indo-American Textbook Program, as it was officially designated, ultimately produced over eight million low-priced reprints of nearly two thousand American university and polytechnic textbooks. Although official data on the amount of rupee funds expended are not available, information gathered from several sources indicates that the eight million textbooks produced during the twenty-year period cost between $16 and $18 million (in rupees)—or a little over $2.00 per copy.

Rupee funds were made available for this purpose under Public Law 480 of the 83d Congress, titled the Agricultural Trade and Development Assistance Act of 1954. This act allowed developing countries to pay for purchases of U.S. surplus agricultural commodities in local currencies rather than in scarce U.S. dollars. Such amounts paid and held in the account of the U.S. government which were determined by the U.S. Department of the Treasury to be in excess of normal needs, such as costs of operating U.S. embassies, could be used for a number of specified purposes, as negotiated with host-country governments, including support for publication and distribution of textbooks and other educational materials. Surplus or excess currencies proposed for such purposes required specific appropriation by the U.S. Congress, just as regular dollar funds do.

The Joint Indo-American Textbook Program was established in response to a formal request of the Indian Ministry of Education (MOE). At the MOE's request, a body was constituted to set policies and to provide administrative oversight for the program.

That body, designated as the Joint Indo-American Textbook Board, was made up of officials of the MOE and USIA. It is worth noting that similar joint boards for Soviet and British low-priced textbook programs were already in existence at that time, and that they still exist today.

Policies established by this board provided for review and approval of textbooks proposed by Indian publishers; for royalties to American publishers not to exceed 10 percent of U.S. list prices and subject to a 50 percent Indian income tax; for printing and binding of the reprint editions *in India;* and for sale to Indian students at one-fifth of the U.S. list prices.

Once a book was approved by the MOE, USIA negotiated a subsidy contract with the Indian publisher. (No contract was signed, however, until the publisher produced a signed translation agreement with the American copyright owner.) Essentially, the USIA contract granted direct subsidy support (normally 80 percent of total production costs and 100 percent of royalty payments) and required the Indian publisher to produce the book within a specified period of time, to price it at the required low list price, and then to promote sales actively.

As the program grew, USIA funding became inadequate to match the increasing requirements. Moreover, USIA questioned whether it should be supporting growing numbers of textbooks in the natural sciences and technology. Its charter was (and is today) to support U.S. foreign policy and to explain American culture and its institutions.

For these reasons, the USAID Mission in India joined the American "side" of the program in 1969 with $6 million in funding support in three installments. Thus, AID became a cosponsor of the Joint Indo-American Textbook Program, taking over funding for all scientific and technical books.

Success of the dual program in India was due in large measure to the fortunate mix of large-scale funding; to careful, professional planning by Indian and American members of the board; and, importantly, to the cooperation of Indian and American publishers. The support given by several joint Indo-American publishing ventures, established during the early years of the program, was also a major factor. At least six U.S. publishers set up these joint-venture firms with Indian partners. These firms provided badly needed editorial experience and managerial skill, and they quickly formed the nucleus of a professionally experienced Indian publishing base. Further, these Indo-American publishers have continued to serve both Indian education and publishing by producing many Indian or Indo-American and coauthored textbooks.

It is significant to note that in the first year of operation, the P.L. 480 Textbook Program sponsored the publication of only 19 reprint editions of American textbooks in some fifty thousand copies. After several years of experience, and with greatly enhanced funding in the late 1960s and the early 1970s, this output was multiplied ten times over. In 1970, the peak year, 297 reprint editions were published in 1.7 million copies. Unfortunately, the Pak-Indo war of 1971 brought a major break in relations between the Indian and American governments. One of the consequences was a sharp decline in funding for the P.L. 480 Textbook Program. Residual funds were used to keep the output reasonably high for a few years. But by the mid-1970s only a small number of reprints was produced each year. It dropped to an all-time low of four titles in 1981 (Appendix E).

Although the P.L. 480 Textbook Program, as described above, may not be the pivotal factor, it is certain that with its decline the import of American books by India has dropped steadily over the past decade. It would appear that the time has arrived to resurrect the program in one form or another.

Association of American University Presses (AAUP). In 1965, this association included almost all university presses of the United States and Canada, plus the National University of Mexico Press. From 1965 to 1976, the AAUP jointly founded and operated with the National University of Mexico an imaginative program in Mexico City known as Centro Interamericano de Libros Academicos (CILA), or Inter-American Scholarly Book Center, as it was called on this side of the border. The highly laudable objectives of this project as stated in part at its founding, were to carry on the following activities:

> 1. *Maintain an extensive exhibit or reference library* of important scholarly books from all American countries and in the various languages of the hemisphere: Spanish, Portuguese, English, and French. ... This collection will be available for use by scholars, booksellers who wish to examine books before ordering them, publishers interested in translation rights, and the general public.

31

2. *Purchase and stock additional copies of many books for sale,* thus conducting a retail bookstore in connection with the Center. (Few scholarly books from the United States and even fewer from other Latin American scholarly publishers are currently available in bookstores.)

3. *Supply books at standard discounts to other bookstores and to libraries,* thus acting as a jobbing agency for publishers who wish to avail themselves of this service. . . . Discounts allowed to dealers will be sufficient to enable them to sell books at the same price at which the Center offers them for sale. . . .

4. *Maintain a complete catalogue and order service* for cooperating publishers so that books not in stock can be obtained. At present, a scholar frequently cannot purchase individual books published outside his own country; problems of credit and exchange and limited or non-existent profit on small orders make this sort of intellectual communication extremely difficult.

5. *Develop customer lists and direct mail selling methods throughout Latin America.* Direct mail, so common in Europe and the United States (and indeed the chief method of selling specialized scholarly books), has been little used in Latin America. . . .

6. *Work toward the development of a Latin American version of "Scholarly Books in America.* Published by AAUP, it is a complete quarterly descriptive bibliography of all books published by member presses in the United States and Canada. Its regular free distribution to libraries and scholars enables them to learn quickly about books of interest to them.

7. *Prepare lists and catalogues of books published in Spanish and Portuguese* by Latin American scholarly publishers and utilize the Educational Directory (the cooperative mailing service of AAUP) to distribute these lists to interested scholars and libraries in the United States and Canada.

8. *Sell Latin American books directly by mail to scholars and libraries* in the United States and Can-

ada. It will be an enormous boon to Latin American-
ists in this country to have a dependable source of
supply for scholarly books from Latin America. . . .

9. *Provide informal advice on scholarly publishing*
and on the establishment of university presses to
Latin American institutions which desire it.

10. *Assist publishers to obtain translation rights to
scholarly books* which they wish to publish in their
own languages, or at least to help them find out who
should be approached in connection with such rights.

From the start, CILA operated under the governance of a
joint board of directors, of which the Mexican members were
appointed by the rector of the National University, the U.S. members by the AAUP. The executive director and the assistant director were appointed, respectively, in the same way, and both performed knowledgeably and competently—and to the satisfaction
of the book trade of both North and South America. Further, the
nonsales activities and services of the center proved to be of great
value to hundreds of scholars and librarians in both Anglo-America and Ibero-America, and especially so to those of Mexico. And,
to the surprise of many, CILA's sale of Spanish/Portuguese books
to Anglo-America outstripped its sale of English-language books
to Ibero-America. Quite clearly, this indicated that most Latin
American publishers of scholarly books had not known how to
exploit ready markets for their products in the United States and
Canada.

In spite of its auspicious early operations, CILA soon encountered financial difficulty. Its start-up costs had been financed by
grants from the Ford Foundation and the Rockefeller Foundation
to the University of Texas, which acted as the center's fiscal
agent. The two grants, made in January 1964, totaled $320,000.
This amount was supposed to cover operating deficit for four
years; after that CILA was projected to be self-supporting. But
this was not to be.

By the end of the second year of operations (1967), the central
problem could be identified: The revenue-producing activities
were not bringing in enough income to pay their own expenses
and that of the nonrevenue activities as well. But both the board
and the executive director felt that CILA was honor-bound to
continue the purely service activities to which it was committed.
This resulted, naturally, in a squeeze on budgets for sales ex-

pense. So the project struggled on for several years with deficit spending while the AAUP was seeking additional supporting grants. None was forthcoming, but in 1969 and 1971 the two original grantors gave additional grants totaling $55,000 for the "orderly termination" of the center.

On reading the several reports of the AAUP delegations and specialists who went to Mexico to investigate the problems of CILA, one has to reach certain hard conclusions.

First, it was planned on a scale that was far too broad and too costly for its start-up fund and its potential operating income. It attempted to do too much with too little of both money and staff.

Second, there was a fairly sharp and enervating difference in basic concepts of purpose between the two partners in the venture. The Mexican side appeared to think that the services to scholars and scholarship were the main purpose of the center, while the AAUP side seemed to look upon an increase in two-way sales of scholarly books as the principal goal. This difference kept the two sides from working in close harmony, particularly in the matter of budgeting operating expense.

Third, although CILA was a failure, its history indicates that a more simply structured and directed similar organization probably could succeed in substantially increasing the flows of scholarly books between the two Americas on a self-supporting basis. We suggest that this is something for the new generation of university press directors to think about.

Government Advisory Committee on Book and Library Programs (GAC). Although a history of this now defunct body may not fit neatly under the rubric of this part of our report, the purpose and accomplishments of GAC should be described here if for no reason other than the value of such a summary as critical observation alone. Certainly, the fifteen years of the committee's operation brought many benefits and taught many cautionary lessons that should be remembered and valued for years to come.

GAC was established in 1962 under the authority of the Fulbright-Hayes Act. It functioned beneficially until 1977, when it fell victim to President Carter's edict on the abolishment of all "nonessential" government advisory groups. Its demise was a sore disappointment to scores of people who had observed the committee's very useful function at very low cost to the government. All members had served without compensation, and its operating expense, including that of a small secretariat (two persons), had been shared by USIA, AID, and the Bureau of Educational and Cultural Affairs. It had no operating programs or projects. Its sole function was to review and advise on proposed or ongoing programs by federal agencies—a fact that was not understood, most unfortunately, either by the book industry generally or within some of the government agencies that were involved.

Actually, even the genesis of GAC was the result of a fundamental misunderstanding. Attorney General Robert Kennedy made a speech at the 1961 annual meeting of the American Booksellers Association (ABA). He (or perhaps one of his speechwriters) had read an article by a book publisher which deplored the lack of communication and rapport between the book industry and the officials who planned and managed the government's major overseas book programs. The publisher had urged the need for an advisory committee that would meet regularly and serve as a conduit for more information and better understanding between the book industry and the government bureaucrats. In his ABA address, Bobby Kennedy quoted the publisher's suggestion and heartily endorsed the idea of organizing such an advisory committee. This endorsement was loudly applauded by his audience.

Immediately after the ABA meeting Kennedy asked Ed Murrow, the director of USIA at the time, to follow through. Murrow, then well advanced in a fatal illness, passed the assignment along to his deputy director, Donald Wilson, who was on leave from his regular job as general manager of Time, Inc. Thereupon, Wilson asked the cited publisher to come to Washington for an informal discussion. It was then that the fundamental misunderstanding was discovered. Kennedy had thought he was endorsing the idea of a committee of government officials who would advise commercial publishers on how and where to sell U.S. books in the developing countries of the world. And he was particularly interested in ways and means for distributing more Government Printing Office publications abroad.

In spite of the initial misunderstanding, it did not take long for the book publisher and the magazine publisher cum bureaucrat to agree that the need for advice ran much more to the government's side. They agreed, too, that a committee of publishers and booksellers should be organized forthwith. Accordingly, the two conferees soon drew up an operational plan and nominated prospective members, all of which was quickly approved by Director Murrow and by Dean Rusk, then secretary of state.

GAC's first meeting was held in the fall of 1962 with a membership of twelve publishers and booksellers, appointed formally by Secretary Rusk for rotating three-year terms. From the start, the committee reported to the secretary through the assistant secretary for cultural and educational affairs, and it had official liaison with the director of USIA and AID. It was originally concerned with book programs only. A few years later, the committee was enlarged to include librarians and its name was changed accordingly. Appointed in addition were government observers from some eight or ten other agencies that had minor interests in overseas book programs. Also, the directors of the American Library Association, the American Book Publishers Council (one of the predecessor organizations of the Association of American Publishers), the American Booksellers Association, the Association of American University Presses, and the Information Industry Association were designated as appointed observers.

During the first two years, the committee met with its Washington constituency every other month, and thereafter it met quarterly.

It should be emphasized that GAC was never given an official agenda, neither did it have any authority for taking decisions or making formal recommendations. Its sole mission was to review and advise on projects and problems that were brought to it by its constituent government agencies. And it did review all major programs that were conducted overseas, and it did cause many seemingly unsound proposals to be canceled. Further, while serving in this "watchdog" capacity in Washington, it kept interested book publishers and librarians currently informed on governmental policies, plans, and actions that they should know about.

So much for the formal side of GAC's function. On the informal side, it set about several more subtle tasks. First, it tried to encourage all federal agencies to use the committee meetings as an information clearinghouse and an open forum for discussion and debate. Second, it tried to get all agencies to adopt uniform policies and practices in their dealings with publishers and the book trade. Third, it tried to get the major agencies to formalize their policies and practices in written statements for the benefit of the committee and of their own staffs in Washington and abroad. Fourth, it tried to get USIA and USAID to adopt a single, unified set of policies and practices for their separate dealings with suppliers of services at home and with the foreign-government recipients of their aid abroad. Although these informal tasks were pursued doggedly for years by certain GAC members, almost nothing was accomplished by their efforts. It seemed that most agency directors preferred at heart to remain free to go their own ways with as little regulation as possible. Another serious hindrance was the frequent turnover of top administrative offices in most of the agencies. It is a matter of record that in its first three years, GAC's liaison with USIA and AID was with eleven different directors or assistant directors. Indeed, a few of the more fleeting of these officials were not in their jobs long enough to gain more than remote familiarity with the purpose and the responsibility of the committee. But then, as now, this seemingly constant change had to be accepted as a way of life in Washington. Most agencies, however, were fortunate enough to have more stability in their second and third echelons of career administrators. They provided the necessary experience and continuity to keep operations going without too much interruption or uncertainty.

Most of the old-timers who served as members of GAC now agree that, despite its difficulties and limitations, the committee had several desirable effects beyond its routine meeting-to-meeting performance.

—It clearly demonstrated the benefits of the continuous exchange of information and the sharing of experience among its constituent agencies.

—It educated many publishers and librarians in the ways and requisites of governmental operations.

—It provided its members with enlightening insights to how government policy is formulated and manipulated.

—It educated dozens of government administrators in the economics of publishing, with particular reference to production costs and distribution problems.

—It caused certain reforms of government contracting and procurement procedures that were of considerable benefit on both sides.

—It helped to check certain dishonest and costly cheating practices that were all too often prevalent and customary at the receiving end of assistance programs in many countries.

—It helped alert U.S. book publishers and librarians to the urgent need for expert technical assistance to developing countries in building their indigenous book industries and library systems.

37

—It constantly reminded the State Department of its first-line responsibility for protection against copyright infringement and book "piracy" abroad and for active encouragement of universal adherence to one or another of the several international copyright conventions.

—It saved literally millions of U.S. taxpayers' dollars by advising against the start of new assistance projects or for the cancellation of older ones that were, patently, too ineffectual or costly for the benefits promised or realized.

An experienced observer might well say that any one of these benefits probably was worth all the government's costs and all the private efforts that went into GAC's operation. But how can such things be measured for either short-term or long-term benefits?

One thing, however, can be said for sure: Many people who were involved with GAC have been pleased that USIA appointed last year a new Book and Library Committee that will, perhaps, be able to carry on where GAC left off in 1977.

PART 6

Current U.S. Assistance Programs

In recent years, no new export assistance program of large size has been inaugurated as a replacement for any of the past programs that have been described. And most of the few programs that have survived, both public and private, have wasted away—withered on the vine—for want of financial support and aggressive direction. In fact, very few still have sufficient substantive worth to justify more than a summary mention in this report.

Government Agencies and Commissions

The United States Information Agency (USIA). This important but often neglected federal agency underwent a mutation for a short period, 1973 to 1983, when its functions were combined with the Bureau of Educational and Cultural Affairs in the State Department. The amalgam was given a new name, International Communications Agency. The old name was restored in late 1982, however, and the independence and the legislated purpose of the agency has since remained unchanged.

As in past years, the USIA continues to be responsible for conducting informational, educational, cultural, and other related exchange programs between the United States and other nations. It currently maintains 201 posts in 125 countries. Support for book and library programs is one important means by which USIA fulfills its mission of increasing "mutual understanding between the people of the United States and the people of other countries." Major efforts include assistance in book publication, translation, and promotion, plus the administration of United States Information Services (USIS) libraries throughout the world.

Since 1950 USIA has assisted publications of books on U.S. foreign policy, political and social processes, economy, science and technology, education, and the arts and humanities. Through September 1980, the agency had assisted in the overseas production of more than twenty-three thousand editions totaling more than

39

181 million copies in fifty-seven languages, including English. At the present time, USIA's dwindling book programs work mainly in the following languages: Arabic, Chinese, French, Portuguese, and Spanish. Small programs continue in Bengali, Burmese, Japanese, Korean, Malay, Thai, and Turkish.

The agency currently maintains 131 libraries of various kinds in 79 countries. They are known locally by such names as American Cultural Center, American Library, USIS Library, Amerika Haus, or Biblioteca Abraham Lincoln. The agency also lends support to libraries located in binational centers (autonomous local institutions dedicated to the development of mutual understanding between the United States and the host country). Although the nature of the libraries does vary from country to country according to local needs and conditions, they generally include collections of books, periodicals, documents, and audiovisual materials, and they offer a variety of services that would not otherwise be available in the host countries. USIS librarians also maintain close contact with libraries and other cultural and educational institutions in the host countries. In 1981, USIA expenditures for library materials and services totaled $3.5 million, including $1.5 million for books alone.

The peak year of USIA-"sponsored" production of books was 1965, when a total of almost 13 million copies were printed for all language editions. In 1977, production had dropped to a total of fewer than one million copies, and it has, alas, remained well below that level to this date.

Appendix F displays a historical record of the numbers of copies of translated or reprinted editions assisted in whole or in part by the USIA since the agency's inception. The numbers apparently include copies produced in the Low-Priced Books programs (both textbook and Ladder Series editions) and in the various P.L. 480 reprint and translation programs and probably those in the many translated-book series produced by Franklin Book Programs, but USIA has no clear record of what is included in this compilation. It can be assumed, however, that the U.S. government did not pay a good part of the total cost of the 151.5 million copies produced under the USIA aegis.

Currently, U.S. government policy is to induce the private sector to check the sharp decline in the USIA-assisted book programs for developing countries. Looking at the matter realistically, one has to question whether this policy can possibly be implemented with more than minimal success, even though there are signs of general economic recovery in the offing. Yet, there appears to be no doubting the argument that, at this particular time, public policy does need much more private-sector support than it has had in the past.

Peace Corps (PC). Through its Information Collection and Exchange Center (ICE), the Peace Corps collects, reviews, and catalogs training and educational materials for use by its overseas field staffs. Also, it produces technical manuals and distributes them in large quantities; seven of them were printed and widely distributed in 1980 on such subjects as agriculture, fisheries, forestry, conservation, and community health. In addition, it buys specialized manuals from U.S. commercial publishers and uses others supplied by various related government agencies.

National Library of Medicine (NLM). This monumental information center operates a Literature Exchange Program with approximately four hundred partners in seventy-two countries throughout the world. It deals largely in bibliographic publications and other kinds of secondary information service. It also has a Special Foreign Currency Program that operates under Public Law 83-480, which allows the use of surplus P.L. 480 funds to finance scientific writing projects in seven cooperating countries: Israel, Poland, Yugoslavia, Egypt, Tunisia, India, and Pakistan. During 1980 there were ninety-five active projects in this program.

Library of Congress (LC). Among the many informational activities of the Library of Congress are two that are especially relevant to this study. The first is a large mutual exchange program with ninety-two foreign governments, which serves some 13,500 libraries and other educational and research institutions. About 1.4 million U.S. publications are distributed abroad annually under this worldwide program. The second is the Center for the Book, a promotional organization that is housed and partly staffed by the Library but largely financed by private-sector contributions. This relatively new public-private collaboration is dedicated to the enhancement of the general welfare of books and their creators and to wider distribution and use of books at home and abroad. Its purpose and various pro bono publico activities have set a new pattern of government and private-sector cooperation that could have, with sufficient support, far-reaching consequences. The center's sponsorship of the present study is typical of its current activity. In short, it can be assumed that in time the

41

center's influence will be far more important than its currently limited affluence.

Intergovernmental Agencies

Organization of American States (OAS). The Organization of American States is an international organization established to strengthen the peace and security of the Western Hemisphere and to promote the economic, social, scientific, educational, and cultural development of its member states (of which there were twenty-seven in 1981). The magazine *Revista Interamericana de Bibliografia,* published by the OAS since 1951, is a source of information on books from or about Latin America or the Caribbean. It includes book reviews, notes about authors, notices of important meetings, and reports of research in progress. Also, it lists new U.S. government publications about Latin America.

The book, library, and publishing projects sponsored by the OAS Department of Cultural Affairs focus on promoting literacy, developing materials for young readers and for new adult readers, improving book distribution, assisting libraries, and encouraging cooperation among all parts of the book community. Several of the major projects can be described briefly.

The Inter-American Project on Children's Literature was established in 1978 by the OAS Department of Cultural Affairs to improve the textual and visual quality of books, to aid in their distribution and lower their cost, and to increase the world market for Latin American children's books. The project sponsors training for authors, illustrators, and publishers, and it has created a network of documentation centers for children's literature throughout Spanish-speaking Latin America.

Between 1977 and 1981, the OAS Department of Cultural Affairs funded two projects, one in El Salvador and one in Colombia, both aimed at developing ways to disseminate printed information to low-level adult readers in poverty areas. Using experience thus gained, the department has financed a program in 1982–83 in Guatemala, Honduras, and Nicaragua that will seek in each country to coordinate publishing and information activities relating to low-income populations.

United Nations Educational, Scientific, and Cultural Organization (UNESCO). Book development has been an important objective of this well-known organization since its inception. Its activities have included guidance to developing countries in expanding book production, promotion of the free flow of books throughout the world, publication of studies and reports on regional and national book needs, and the regulation and monitoring of international copyright problems and practices. The main objective is to assist all countries to achieve an adequate level of book production, always viewing books as part of a larger, interrelated cultural program.

UNESCO's publishing program includes dozens of items relating to books and book development. *Book Promotion News*, a quarterly bulletin, carries news of regional activities, book fairs and exhibitions, and recent publications. Among its monographic series, Books about Books, inaugurated in 1979, is of special interest.

The general conference of UNESCO proclaimed 1972 as International Book Year "to focus the attention of the general public [and of] governments and international and domestic organizations on the role of books and related materials in the lives and affairs of the individual and society." A program resulting from the experience and suggestions garnered during the year was published in a booklet, *Books for All*, which aimed at promoting "world-wide action in favor of books and reading." In 1982 UNESCO sponsored a World Congress on Books to assess developments since the International Book Year and prepare recommendations for future UNESCO programs.

Pan-American Health and Education Foundation (PAHEF). Although this is technically an independent, nonprofit private-sector organization (incorporated and based in Washington, D.C.), its initial funding came in 1970 from a low-interest loan from the Inter-American Development Bank. In later years, this funding has been supplemented by substantial donations by a few U.S. foundations and corporations. But by making careful use of revolving funds, the corporation's book program has been largely self-supporting.

The Medical Book Program was originally conceived by the Pan-American Health Organization (PAHO), with which the public service directors of the foundation have worked closely in assisting universities and medical schools in twenty-nine Latin American countries. Actually, the foundation was created because the Inter-American Development Bank could not legally make a loan to another international agency such as the PAHO. The amount of the first loan in 1970 was U.S. $2 million for the medical education program. This program was so successful that it was extended in 1973 to nursing education, an even more needy area.

The need and the operating principles for the original medical book program had been rationalized by the foundation's directors as follows:

> The fact that textbooks in Spanish and Portuguese were not within the economic reach of medical students adversely affected the teaching-learning process. . . .
>
> The goal, then, was to facilitate acquisition of books while students were still in medical school, and in the process to encourage physicians to accumulate their own basic reference libraries.
>
> Analysis of the problem led to a proposal for a revolving fund which could provide the capital needed to conduct direct negotiations with publishers—either for purchase of books in quantity or for the right to print them independently. By operating on a nonprofit basis, holding down administrative costs, limiting the number of books included in the program, and making each school responsible for sales, storage, and record-keeping, books could be made available to students at half the regular market price. Cooperation, or at least tacit acceptance, by local bookstores could be encouraged by systematically restricting the program to undergraduate medical students and not opening it to practitioners.

By 1977 the book programs had far exceeded the goals established in the original loan agreement. Rights to translate twenty-eight textbooks into Spanish and Portuguese had been purchased from U.S. publishers, and 335,000 copies of the translated editions had been sold through 146 participating schools. At that time, the foundation reported that the publishers involved had cooperated fully and had been pleased with the results. Also, it pointed out that PAHEF had expanded the demand for books among groups that previously had bought none at all. In effect, the programs had "made the market," so that publishers were able to produce in larger volume at lower costs.

Also reported was the fact that the foundation had purchased more than half of its supply of books as regular editions of U.S. publishers and fewer than half had been purchased as licensed translations.

In the wake of the successes with the medical and nursing programs, the foundation's assistance was extended to the training of the entire health team, including the technicians, auxiliaries, and community health workers who were so necessary to serve remote populations that had never been adequately served in the past. This wider expansion was made possible by an additional loan of U.S. $5 million by the Inter-American Development Bank.

From every point of view—that of international public financing, of private-sector governance and management, and of cost-effectiveness in filling critical needs—PAHEF can be taken as a model for similar organizations to assist educational programs in other professional and occupational areas such as agriculture, engineering, forestry, conservation, communications, and behavioral science.

U.S. Private Organizations

The Asia Foundation. This is probably the oldest and the most consistently effective of all the private organizations of its kind in America. Founded in 1954, the foundation has its main office in San Francisco and a branch office in Washington, D.C. Its board of directors is composed of nationally prominent members who have served well to guide the foundation's several operating programs and to help in keeping them financially solvent.

Books for Asia is one of the larger divisions of the foundation. At November 1, 1982, it had shipped 20 million U.S. books to educational and cultural institutions of twenty-two Asian countries. (See Appendix G for a cumulative record of its donations of books and journals for the years 1954–82.)

The Books for Asia's home operating budget has averaged between $300,000 and $400,000 per annum in recent years. In addition, from $600,000 to $700,000 has been supplied annually by the foundation's central budget for such expenses as offshore shipping, staffing and maintaining the overseas distribution centers, and a share of overhead expenses. For many years, the USIA has heavily financed the offshore shipping costs.

More specifically, during fiscal 1981, Books for Asia sent 636,000 books and journals to seventeen Asian and Pacific Island countries. This total was about 24 percent less than the amount shipped in FY 1980. The decline can be explained in part by a decrease in book donations as well as by problems experienced in shipping books to particular countries. Actually, four out of every five books sent to Asia are donated. In 1981, Books for Asia accepted donations of 517,000 books with a value of $4.6 million.

45

Over 60 percent of them came from U.S. publishers.

A 1979 IRS ruling concerning publishers' inventory tax (based on the "Thor Power Tools" case) has affected the pattern of publishers' donations. There was a 28 percent reduction in donations from 1980 to 1981, a decline from 409,000 to 327,000 copies.

Another factor affected the quantity of books donated by publishers in 1981. Many American firms are expanding their sales efforts in Asia, and hence they are becoming increasingly reluctant to donate books to the foundation, for fear of injuring their own sales. In the future, it will be necessary to accept restrictions on the ultimate destination of books donated by publishers. It appears that these restrictions are not likely to affect book programs in the People's Republic of China, however, or those in certain countries of South Asia.

In addition to donations, Books for Asia purchases material for overseas shipment. A primary source of these purchases is the American textbook wholesalers (who also donate tens of thousands of books each year). During 1981, Books for Asia expanded its contacts in this area, thus ensuring the steady flow of high-quality used books (making up, in part, for the decline in new book donations from publishers).

Books for Asia had several notable successes in 1981. Most significant, perhaps, was the dramatic increase in books shipped to the People's Republic of China (PRC): 18,900 volumes, as opposed to 4,853 in 1980. Further, book shipments to Sri Lanka increased threefold in fiscal 1981, from 15,639 to 48,768. And in the Republic of the Maldives, Books for Asia sent the first general shipment of 5,901 volumes. This single shipment more than doubled that country's supply of books.

Shipments to Bangladesh were increased by 35 percent in 1981. The majority of these shipments were sent to the foundation's office in Dacca for general distribution. Toward the end of the fiscal year, however, large numbers of requests were received from Dacca for special collections for particular institutions.

It is anticipated that the appointment of a resident foundation representative in Pakistan will lead to a solution of the problem of customs restrictions on the importation of books, which will enable Books for Asia to increase distribution in that country.

A final "success" was the Malaysia program. The quantity of books shipped increased by 62 percent, to 44,839, making Malaysia the fifth largest program in Asia for the year. Of special interest is the fact that a substantial portion of the books sent to Malaysia was composed of special collections for particular institutions, such as the Bintulu Development Authority and the University of Malaya.

Under present conditions, given the drastic reduction or the elimination of so many federal assistance programs, the Asia Foundation can be taken as a prototype and model for the initiation of other private-sector organizations of the same sort as "gap-filling" efforts. Several such organizations do now exist, but none of them approach Books for Asia, either in size or in effective aid to their chosen areas. In fact, the Asia Foundation has pioneered a track that may be not only the best but the *only* way in which other private area-interested groups or corporations or individuals can hope to make a dent in the needs, even the minimal needs, of the many developing countries that deserve U.S. assistance.

The Brother's Brother Foundation (BBF). This Pittsburgh-based philanthropic foundation was established in 1958 as a medical service organization. In recent years its education program has expanded to include a major book distribution program. BBF specializes in assistance by "gifts in kind," and its work is carried on largely by volunteers. Its total program expenditure in 1981 was approximately $4.2 million. Over 95 percent of its financial support comes from private sources.

Most American publishers readily donate overstocks and remainders of superseded editions to countries that are too poor to buy all the books they need. Between 1981 and 1983, BBF shipped nearly four million books donated by American publishers. Most of its book donations go to the Caribbean and four small English-speaking countries in Africa, but in 1982 a significant program was undertaken in the People's Republic of China.

As its book program budget is under $100,000 a year, BBF relies on indigenous institutions in the recipient nations to help cover shipping costs and handle local distribution. Local recipients include government agencies, universities, religious organizations, and civic groups. BBF also solicits, packs, and ships book donations for other charities, including the Asia Foundation, the Foundation for Books to China, and the Pan American Development Foundation.

The Foundation for Books to China. The Foundation for Books to China, based in San Francisco, has focused its efforts on the People's Republic of China and works in cooperation with UNI-

47

CEF, the U.S. Information Agency, and private agencies such as Project Hope, a distributor of privately donated medical textbooks. Since its creation in 1980, the foundation has shipped approximately five hundred thousand books to China. With help from subsidized ocean freight rates from American President Lines, the foundation expects to continue to ship substantial numbers of U.S. books abroad. Currently all distribution in China is handled by various government agencies and UNICEF representatives.

Association of American University Presses (AAUP). At present, seventy-two North American and four overseas presses are members of this organization. Its purpose is to sponsor workshops, seminars, exhibits, and other similar activities that promote the welfare of university press publishing and the sale of scholarly books in both domestic and overseas markets.

In 1960 an International Cooperation Committee was established. This committee organized and guided the *Centro Interamericano de Libros Academicos* (CILA) project (described in Part 5) from 1965 to its demise in 1976. More recently its members participated in an international conference on scholarly publishing jointly sponsored by UNESCO and the University of Toronto Press that led to the establishment of the International Association of Scholarly Publishers (IASP). The AAUP has continued to foster IASP, as well as supporting specific scholarly presses in other parts of the world, through consultation and by acting as host and coordinator for visiting scholarly publishers from offshore. Through its for-profit marketing-service subsidiary, American University Press Services, the AAUP also conducts cooperative exhibits of its members' books at international scholarly meetings and book fairs. American University Press Services also conducts a program of cooperative advertising projects directed to scholarly and institutional offshore markets.

Children's Book Council, Inc. (CBC). This organization was founded in 1945, as a not-for-profit association dedicated to promoting children's books. Its membership consists of more than seventy U.S. publishers of children's trade books. One of its major promotions is the annual Children's Book Week in November. The organization's publications, including *Calendar, Prelude,* and Children's Book Week promotional materials, are of interest primarily to persons in the United States and Canada.

The council's active international program includes serving, with the Association for Library Service to Children of the American Library Association, as the U.S. National Section of the International Board of Books for Young People (IBBY). The council acts as the U.S. secretariat for IBBY. In this capacity it supports the participation in IBBY affairs of one children's book publisher who serves on IBBY's executive committee; and it administers the participation of Americans in IBBY congresses. Also, it sponsored International Children's Book Day in 1972 and organized Friends of IBBY, Inc., in the United States.

The CBC administers a program of deposits of children's books in countries around the world. For several years the council donated annual deposits of children's books to collections in Third World countries.

National Research Council (NRC). This quasi-governmental organization serves as an operating agency for the National Academy of Sciences and the National Academy of Engineering, private societies of distinguished scholars that advise the federal government in matters of science and technology. The NRC's international work is carried out by the Commission on International Relations, as well as by an advisory committee on the USSR and Eastern Europe, by the Committee on Scholarly Communication with the People's Republic of China, and through the administration of International Atomic Energy Agency Fellowships.

The Board on Science and Technology for International Development (BOSTID) of the NRC conducts studies that both examine development problems of concern to a number of developing nations and suggest ways in which U.S. scientific and technical resources can help solve these problems. Additional studies, generated by BOSTID's Advisory Committee on Technology Innovation (ACTI), concentrate on innovative uses of technologies, plants, and animals in developing countries. The Agency for International Development provides the primary financial support for BOSTID studies.

The World Bank-Philippine Government Textbook Project. This is another intergovernmental program that should be described because it can have a large, long-range impact on U.S.-Philippine relations in general and on a fading export market for U.S. books in particular.

In a sense, this project picked up, in a more realistic way, where the failed USAID-Philippine project left off in 1975. The current project was planned largely by an experienced American consulting firm which has also monitored its progress. To date, it has managed, apparently, to avoid the major mistakes that crippled the earlier USAID program.

The present jointly financed project was planned in two phases: Phase I to run from 1976 to 1981, and Phase II from 1982 to 1985. Phase I was budgeted at U.S. $50 million for the production of 27 million textbooks and accompanying teachers' editions. Actually, 35.6 million copies of eighty-three titles were produced and distributed by August 1982. Phase II was also budgeted at U.S. $50 million for four years, but planned for the production of 11 million textbooks and teachers' editions *per year* over a ten-year period. The World Bank will be involved in cofinancing for four years only, however. To date some 50 million copies of new texts and second editions of Phase I texts have been produced in Phase II. Presumably, the Philippine government will be able to carry on without further World Bank financial assistance after 1985.

The terms and conditions for financing both phases of this program require the World Bank to supply hard-currency loans of 50 percent of the budgets for the purchase of foreign publishing rights and manufacturing materials, while the Philippine government pays 50 percent in its own peso soft currency to pay local salaries and other operating and distributing costs.

The project is operated by a Textbook Board Secretariat, a publishing organization responsible to the Ministry of Education. The board was set up under a concept of "institutional building" as well as a policy and management authority. This is to say that its mandate was to use a systems approach in its task of supplying free textbooks for all Filipino elementary and high school students. This has resulted in the building of a professional staff of more than one hundred specialists in the various aspects of publishing—editing, testing, design, manufacturing, quality control, and distribution. Also, emphasis has been placed on an intensive teacher-training program that helps to introduce the new textbooks in classrooms.

Phase I of the project concentrated, quite naturally, on elementary texts on fundamental subjects ("the three R's") in the native languages. Phase II has concentrated on high school texts with special emphasis on mathematics, natural science, social science, and the language arts (the several Philippine languages and English as a second language).

In passing, it should be mentioned that, in addition to the successful Philippine program, the World Bank is financing, on similar patterns, several developing national-textbook projects in Africa and Asia, and to a lesser extent in Latin America. In all cases commercial publishers are helping and are benefiting both directly and indirectly. British and French publishers have been working closely with the World Bank on these new projects, but, strangely enough, U.S. book publishers have shown very little interest in them. Perhaps it is a question of long-term versus short-term outlooks.

PART 7

Assistance Programs
of Other Countries

As noted earlier, other industrialized countries have stepped up their national programs for assistance to book exports, while U.S. programs have been on the decline. Political, commercial, cultural, and humanitarian purposes have been combined in various proportions in all instances. And in all instances national governments have supplied the main initiatives and most of the required financing. In the USSR, where by far the largest effort has been made, only the central government or the constituent republics have been involved, there being no private sector.

A look at the assistance programs of five of the larger book-publishing countries (all competitors of the United States) can be helpful here in several ways.

—We can learn concepts and methods that might be used to strengthen our own faltering efforts.

—We can observe that their gains in some places—and particularly in developing countries—are inimical to our own interests.

—We may have our traditional competitive spirit stimulated and revived.

Soviet Union. An unpublished government report estimates that the total USSR propaganda effort is at present seven times larger than that of the United States. This report calculates that the Soviet Union spends the equivalent of $3.3 billion annually on propaganda activities, including Radio Moscow's foreign service ($700 million), the Communist party's international activities ($150 million), and TASS, the Soviet news agency, which spends $550 million a year advancing Moscow's interpretation of world events.

A report prepared by the USIA research staff in 1981 offers the following insights into Soviet cultural and information activities.

—Soviet efforts are the most intense and diverse in Sub-Saharan Africa and South Asia; less in Latin America, the Near East, North Africa, and Western Europe; and least in East Asia.

—Among the countries where the USSR is most active are: all Sub-Saharan African nations; India, Mexico, Nicaragua, and Peru; Algeria, Jordan, and Syria; Austria, Cyprus, Finland, Greece, Italy, and Spain; and Japan and the Philippines.

—The Soviets appear to concentrate more on scholarships and academic or professional exchanges and on getting their viewpoint into local media than on films, trade fairs and exhibits, cultural exhibits and presentations, and cultural centers or friendship societies.

—Although academic and cultural exchange are concentrated in nations of Sub-Saharan Africa, Latin America, and South Asia, media propaganda programs are much more widespread.

The report also describes more specifically the book activities administered by the Soviets in Sub-Saharan Africa.

—Soviet books abound at low cost in bookstores throughout Africa. Many are translated into English or French and some into an African vernacular. Translated editions usually are produced in the USSR; few translations are published locally elsewhere. The books generally deal with Communist ideology, scientific and technical subjects, life and the arts in the USSR, and children's interests. Some books in Russian are distributed in Africa, usually for language-teaching purposes.

—Soviet book distributors have concentrated their efforts on university bookstores, taking advantage of the scarcity and high cost of textbooks from the West. Soviet book donations to university, secondary school, and public libraries and to government offices are usually generous and frequent. Libraries at Soviet cultural centers, notably in Ghana, tend to give books away free. In many countries, local Communist party organizations give Soviet books freely to radically inclined students and teachers.

Soviet media-related activity, such as press releases and periodical and book distribution, is by far the greatest in India.

—Large numbers of pro-Soviet newspapers and magazines are circulated in India. Fifty publications are put out by the Communist party of India alone.

—The Soviet foreign-trade organization Mezhdunarodnaia Kniga ("International Books") manages an extensive distribution system for the import and sales of Soviet publications.

Books are inexpensive, indicating a large Soviet subsidy. Along with Soviet periodicals, they are sold chiefly in the many Communist-owned or sponsored bookstores. (People's Publishing House, for example, has a network of bookstores that covers all major cities and many towns.) Over five hundred Soviet book titles are imported annually, and about one hundred translations of Soviet books into Indian languages are published each year.

—Twenty-three Soviet periodicals (mostly in English) are sent to subscribers and other recipients in India through USSR Information Offices. Circulation figures are sizable—80,000 for *Soviet Woman*, 75,000 for *New Times*. In addition, the Soviet Embassy's Information Department publishes seven periodicals in forty-nine editions, including English- and twelve vernacular-language editions. Their combined print run in 1978 exceeded twenty million copies.

The Soviets also maintain a high level of activity in Latin America.

—Soviet books and pamphlets are readily available to those who want them, at least in the capital cities. Most outlets are private bookstores, usually located near universities. Communist and revolutionary parties frequently run their own bookstores. For example, in Peru there are two or three chains of bookstores run by the Peruvian Communist party. Mexico shows the most striking pattern of book distribution, with six bookstores selling Soviet books, plus many bookstands near universities.

—There are twenty-nine Communist-front publishing houses, two of which are directly funded by the Mexican Communist party.

As for the production of foreign-language books in the USSR, two large houses share this assignment. *Mir*, whose name signifies both "world" and "peace" in English, publishes books at all levels in mathematics, science, and engineering. It produces about 250 new titles per year, of which 80 to 90 are in English. In recent years, the size of the English editions has been reported to range from 15,000 copies for basic science or theoretical mathematics to 50,000 to 100,000 copies for popular science books. We have been unable to document annual printing figures for English-language editions, but a reasonable estimate would be two to three million copies.

The other foreign-langauge publishing house is *Progress*, a word signifying the same in English as in Russian. It specializes in social science and literary works and publishes from 140 to 160 books in English each year. Its printings are reported to be much larger than those of Mir, and most are produced to fill direct orders from Mezhdunarodnaia Kniga. It also copublishes many English-language editions with Communist-oriented houses in the "sister socialist" Soviet bloc countries and in several other countries as well. Again, we have no recent reports on total annual printings, but it seems safe to estimate the aggregate of Progress to be at least four to five million copies per year of English editions alone.

In comparing the export of Soviet cultural, educational, and political publications with that of the United States or of any other Western democracy, one should keep in mind several important basic facts.

—The USSR bureaucratic publishing complex operated by Goskomizdat (the State Committee for Publishing, Printing, and the Book Trade, which controls some 137 publishing houses) represents the total output of Soviet books and periodicals. There are no private-sector efforts by commercial publishers, by educational institutions, by professional societies, by trade associations, or by foundations or other philanthropic agencies. Hence, government-to-government comparisons are not valid, even though they do imply measures of national values and intent.

—A large proportion of the English-language books produced by the Soviets are used for instruction in their schools and universities. English is required as a second or third language in all secondary and tertiary educational institutions in every Soviet republic, and students often buy their own English texts and reference books. We have been unable to get a reliable fix on the division between home-use and export of their annual English-language book production, but it stands to reason that home consumption must be quite high—perhaps as high as 50 percent.

—The English-language books produced by Mir and Progress are officially priced at 20 to 40 percent of the prices of counterpart U.S. or British books. Generally, Soviet books are smaller and decidedly inferior in physical quality, but this seems to matter little to the masses of low-income book buyers in less developed countries.

—Mezhdunarodnaia Kniga accepts payments in almost any currency of the world, soft or hard. To be sure, exchange rates are arbitrarily fixed by the USSR, and they customarily are fixed in favor of other communist or socialist countries. The same can be said of terms for credit. Naturally, these factors give the Soviet books a big competitive edge over U.S. books, particularly in Third World countries where U.S. foreign policies and commercial interests are rapidly losing ground.

Great Britain. The principal agency for promoting the sale and use of British books and periodicals overseas is the British Council, which has functioned continuously and effectively since 1934. It is purely a cultural body, an independent government-financed agency, comparable with the B.B.C. Its purpose is stated formally and simply: "The aim of the British Council is to promote an enduring understanding and appreciation of Britain in other countries through cultural, educational and technical cooperation."

The council's eleven programs are guided by continuing private-sector committees, including those for Publishing, Libraries, and English Teaching. Fourteen offices are maintained in the U.K., and eighty offices or operating agencies are located in foreign countries. For fiscal 1982–83, its operating budget was £77.9 million, and it was scheduled to spend £64.2 million of promotional funds provided by other government agencies, mainly by the Overseas Development Agency. Thus, a combined expense budget of £142.1 million was projected for the year.

To knowledgeable outside observers, all the British Council's funds appear to be wisely and well spent. Its programs have solid continuity of planning and management by professionals who are experienced in their assignments. There are no stop-and-go programs and no rapid turnover of political appointees at top executive positions, either at home or abroad. Small wonder, then, that the work of the council goes smoothly and wins favor throughout the world, even in certain countries where the British presence may not be generally welcome.

Following are a few pertinent examples of the council's activities in 1981–82.

—1.7 million books, 8,500 periodicals, and 20,000 films were held in council libraries overseas.

—4.3 million books were produced by the council or with its support.

—272 exhibits of 77,000 books and 3,300 periodicals were sent to seventy-one countries.

—2,200 books were sent for review to specialized journals in thirty overseas countries.

—£1.2 million was spent on book presentations to 805 educational and cultural institutions in ninety-nine developing countries.

—Sixty-four advisers and consultants on British books and libraries were sent on overseas missions.

—163,400 students studied various British-oriented courses at council centers in twenty-nine countries.

—A far larger number of students (263,400) learned English as a second language with council help, either direct or indirect, either in the U.K. or abroad; and over fifteen hundred teachers of English and advisers on methods of teaching English worked overseas during the year.

—The council offered a total of seventeen different courses in English-language teaching, ranging from the simplest of vocational courses to advanced technical courses. Special courses were given for teachers of English from Algeria, France, the Netherlands (two courses), Portugal, Turkey, and the Soviet Union (two courses). Naturally, all this teaching and learning is of English-English, not American-English—a matter of more than surface importance, especially in commerce and industry.

These and other similar cultural and educational activities were carried out by a staff of 3,908, of which 1,434 worked in Britain and 2,474 worked overseas. Considering its organizational stability, its operating policies, its financial resources, and the size and professional competence of its staff, one can readily see why many knowledgeable observers on our side of the Atlantic consider the British Council to be a model national organization for its kind of mission.

Two additional organizations support the promotion of British books overseas, though on a much smaller scale.

The Government Board of Trade gives grants for assisting specialized exhibits and promotional missions that encourage exports to target countries all over the world. These grants usually cover the expense of travel fares only, but not living expenses abroad. Such grants are made to individual participants, whose purpose and performance are strictly monitored. An exhibit has to be certified by a trade association or professional society, and an audit-report must be given after the exhibit is held. For example, all British publishers who exhibit at the Frankfurt Book Fair receive Board of Trade grants, but each has to report the value of business transacted there before allowable expense is reimbursed.

The Book Development Council (B.D.C.) is in effect a division of the Publishers Association (P.A.). It has a full-time director and a small staff who work closely with the British Council and the Board of Trade. (In addition, two full-time officers of the P.A. work almost exclusively for the B.D.C.) The work of the council is organized by a number of regional committees consisting of publishers who are experts in exporting books to particular countries. All work to help their members with day-to-day export problems; they are particularly concerned with controlling credit and currency exchange matters.

There appear to be several reasons why the British are willing to spend so much money and effort on promoting the sale and use of their publications overseas. First, they value their culture and their political institutions very highly, and they consider their books and periodicals to be very effective ambassadors of enlightenment and goodwill to the rest of the world. Second, they have historically had an "export or die" economy; hence they have traditionally exported annually from 40 to 50 percent of their publications. Third, British publishers for many years have worked together selflessly and devotedly for the good of their industry and the general benefit of their common product "the British book," of which they are unanimously and justly proud. Further, British publishers as a rule perceive no cleavage between "literary" books and "non-literary" (or "non-book") books. They publish all kinds with equal enthusiasm and without the fastidious distinctions that are observed by the U.S. book industry. Perhaps the British attitude reflects the influence of their ancient and prestigious university presses, Cambridge and Oxford. To them a book is a book, and each kind of book has its place and value. Fourth, private-sector interests and government agencies have also worked together for years in remarkably close harmony and with clear understanding of mutual interests and objectives.

Fresh evidence of the willingness of the British government to work closely with the country's book industry was given recently by the organization of an informal "All-Party Parliamentary Committee on Publishing." Formed at the instigation of Alexander Macmillan, chairman of Macmillan, Ltd., and Clive Bradley, chief executive of the Publishers Association, the committee proposes to give the book trade "a voice in Parliament," according to a report in the January 29, 1983, issue of the *Bookseller*. Ted Rowlands, a prominent Labour member, chairs the committee, and three other M.P.'s serve as deputy chairmen and secretary. More than thirty additional members pledged their support on the day of the committee's organization. According to the *Bookseller* report, the new group would sometimes be asked to "act as firefighters, to ask questions, to 'bully' Ministers, and help paper over the cracks which can exist between Government departments, and make sure that our problems do not disappear down the drain."

Canada. Considering the size of the Canadian book industry and how much of it is controlled by U.S. and U.K. interests, the Canadian government is very liberal in supporting the industry at home and in promoting its books and authors abroad. This governmental assistance is available mainly to wholly owned or majority-owned Canadian houses, or to individual authors and editors of books that "increase public knowledge and appreciation of Canadian writing." These limitations appear to be inspired by a spirit of nationalism, yet they clearly carry a heavy freight of both cultural and commercial protectionism. Some outside observers have charged that this exclusionary policy smacks of provincialism, even chauvinism; others concede that it is justified on both cultural and commercial grounds. In any case, the policy and its effect have caused some regrettable divisions between the "pure" Canadian houses and the foreign-owned or controlled houses, of which some of the latter have long been domiciled Canadian corporations and are now among the larger publishers of Canadian authors.

The largest instrument of government assistance to publishers and authors is the Canada Council, established in 1957 and patterned, somewhat loosely, on the British Council. It is headed by a twenty-one-member "public interest" board, appointed by the government, as are its director and assistant director. The council reports to Parliament through the minister of communications and is called upon from time to time to appear before parliamentary committes, particularly the House of Commons Standing Committee on Communications and Culture.

Annual block grants from Parliament are the council's main source of funds, but such grants are supplemented by income from a $50 million endowment fund established by Parliament in 1957. The council also received substantial amounts in private donations, usually for specific programs.

Several substantial assistance programs are currently financed and administered by the council. The given fundings were for fiscal 1981–82.

– Block grants to individual publishing houses for general support during the preceding calendar year. Over one hundred such grants were made, twenty-one of them for $25,000 to $68,000.

—Grants to subsidize publication of approved manuscripts. Twenty-one grants were made, ranging from $900 to $16,500.

—Grants for translation of books by Canadian authors into a foreign language other than French. Twenty-five individual grants, ranging from $200 to $23,500.

—Grants to writers and publishers' associations for general book promotion. Twenty-four grants, of which six went to publishers in a total amount of $890,000.

—Grants to "pure" Canadian publishers' associations for general operating expense and for special projects, conferences, and annual meetings. Three grants totaling $149,000.

—Grants to publishers for expenses of promotional tours abroad. Forty grants, ranging from $170 to $20,600, in support of some 120 individual "tourists."

—Grants for the purchase of books by Canadian authors for free distribution at home and abroad by the Association of Canadian Publishers and the Association des éditeurs canadiens. Books at wholesale value of more than $300,000 were bought from 124 majority Canadian-owned houses.

—Grants in support of the annual Canadian National Book Festival. Four grants for different purposes, totaling $265,000.

—Grants to finance public readings by Canadian authors in Canada and in the United States. Approximately four hundred grants totaling no less than $500,000.

In addition to the Canada Council's wide array of assistance programs, several government agencies directly finance and administer specialized programs for the promotion of Canadian books overseas.

The Department of Communications financed two programs that are managed by the Department of Industry, Trade and Commerce. One is the Association for the Export of Canadian Books, which pays from 25 to 57 percent of publishers' costs (not above $15,000 for each house) for mailing catalogs, for free sample copies of textbooks, for space advertising, and so on. The other program finances one half of approved publishers' expenses of attending certain international book fairs for the purpose of selling republication rights. The latter department also helps to finance special projects for the professional development of publishers who are doing business in export markets. Neither of these programs is related to ownership.

The Department of Industry, Trade and Commerce directly finances a program called Export Market Development. It shares the costs of Canadian publishers' trade exploratory trips, of exhibits at international trade fairs, of identification of new markets, of incoming foreign buyers' expense, of organizing export consortia, and so forth. For the period 1971–81, some $40 million was spent in support of this program.

The Department of External Affairs purchases books and periodicals for overseas book centers at Canadian embassies and for schools in developing countries that are introducing new curricula in English and French.

Given the foregoing compilation of evidence, who can doubt that Canadians and their government have proper national pride in their culture and proper appreciation of books as quintessential expressions of the same.

France. The French government has traditionally supported comparatively modest programs for the benefit of overseas libraries and book exports. Such support has been increased, predictably, under the Mitterand government. The budget of the Ministry of Culture (nearly 6 billion francs) was doubled in 1981, and funding for the Book Division of the ministry was tripled in that year. The fund for assistance of book export alone was increased from 26 million to 40 million francs. Further increases were made in 1982. Naturally, most of the available funds for overseas promotion are spent on Francophone African countries.

The Ministry of Culture currently has thirty cultural centers, plus seven branch centers, in thirty-five African countries. Each center has a library with a French book collection ranging from 4,000 to 44,000 volumes. Several of these libraries maintain traveling collections of fifty or more books that are alternated from month to month.

Further, the Ministry of Culture, in collaboration with a number of private-sector organizations, presents books generously to national, municipal, and school libraries in Africa; the total for 1980 was over one million volumes. Most were low-level books of a practical or vocational nature.

The Ministry of Culture also supports a number of departments or agencies for promoting commercial export of books. The largest of these is the Office de Promotion de l'Édition Française (OPEF), which serves as an industry-wide Book Export Council. Members pay only a token membership fee, but they freely supply much guidance and advice on the OPEF's various programs. They organize and manage many general book exhibitions around the world. They print and distribute catalogs, directories, and news bulletins of the book trade. They also organize missions to help in the development of indigenous book publishing in the larger countries of Francophone Africa.

A similar but more specialized organization, the Association Française pour la Diffusion du Livre Scientifique, Technique et Médical (SODEXPORT), also is heavily financed by the Ministry of Culture, as is a still more specialized agency for the promotion of the export of law books (SPELD).

In addition, the Ministry of Culture helps certain individual publishers by giving annual cash grants, on application, for specific promotional schemes overseas. Such assists usually are for promotional efforts in nontraditional markets or for exploratory sales programs of a doubtful or experimental nature.

The Ministry of Foreign Affairs finances an agency called the Association pour la Diffusion de la Pensée Française, which helps the publishing sections of officially organized trade missions to other countries, such as the recent missions to Quebec and to China, where the agency made outright purchases of books and paid the costs of shipping the exhibits. Further, the Foreign Ministry allows its embassies in African countries to make periodic purchases of "suitable" French books for free distribution locally.

The Ministry of Cooperation has an active but rather modest program that subsidizes the purchase or adaptation of French-language textbooks for students in elementary and secondary schools in the former French colonies of Sub-Saharan Africa.

The Ministry of Communications makes an important contribution in allowing all book shipments overseas to go at half the postal rates of other export shipments.

Finally, the Ministry of Foreign Trade, through its agency Compagnie Française d'Assurances pour le Commerce Extérieur

(COFACE), provides insurance at favorable rates for the security of all book export sales.

In 1981, French book exports were 20 percent of total industry sales. (In earlier years, the proportion was as high as 30 percent.) Considering the relatively small size of their export markets and the very low level of purchasing power in most of them, one has to conclude that the current French government is both aggressive and liberal in its promotion of overseas dissemination of its books and other cultural and educational materials.

West Germany. The West German book trade association (Börsenverein), working with the Foreign Ministry, has devised a remarkably simple and effective cooperative way to boost export sales to certain neighboring countries that have special political and commercial importance to the Federal Republic of Germany. The "target" countries are Poland, Czechoslovakia, Hungary, and Bulgaria. Under an arrangement with their Foreign Ministry, the pubishers give extra discounts (which amount to price subsidies) on sales to book dealers in those countries, and the costs of the extra discounts are reimbursed by government payments made through the trade association. The extra-discount allowances are 25 percent on sales to Poland and 15 percent on sales to the other three countries. Thus, if Ars Polona, an official import agency in Warsaw, orders a West German book on which the normal discount is 25 percent, the sale is invoiced at 50 percent. A copy of the invoice is sent to Börsenverein, which periodically collects the amounts due from the Foreign Ministry and makes payments to individual publishers. The purpose of this quite simple arrangement is, of course, to lower consumer prices and thus make the purchase of West German books more attractive. West German publishers report that this marketing strategy has worked smoothly and economically and to the general satisfaction of all concerned. Perhaps the Association of American Publishers and our own State Department should try this German artifice as a way to check the decline of U.S. book sales in certain Third World countries that are of particular importance to us.

PART 8

Deterrents to U.S. Book Exporting

It was stated at the outset that foreign markets are not easily cultivated. In fact, all of them are difficult, and many of them—especially those of developing countries—are as uninviting as briar patches. Now, more specifically, exactly what are these prickly deterrents that are so often encountered? And just where are they the most frequently found?

In order to get well-informed answers to these questions, we identified fourteen deterrents, or impediments, that were suggested by a group of U.S. publishers who are experts at book exporting. Then the largest twenty of our book exporting firms were asked to rate the seriousness of each of the fourteen on a ten point scale—ten points for the most serious, down to one point for the least serious. Thus we derived an opinion poll that we hope is based on thorough knowledge of the problem and as dependable as possible. The results are presented below in rank order, together with comments on the countries or areas where each deterrent is considered to be a serious factor.

1. *A general lack of hard-currency exchange;* not enough to import the essentials of life, much less books, which are considered luxuries. All developing countries of South and Central America, Southeast Asia, and most of Africa. India, Pakistan, Burma, Argentina, and Nigeria were named as currently particular problem countries. (Rated 8.0)

2. *Official limitations placed on hard-currency exchange for books and similar products;* some exchanges available, but other kinds of imports take precedence. Here China, Thailand, Nigeria, Brazil, Chile, India, and the Philippines were named. (Rated 7.8)

3. *Comparatively high prices of U.S. books.* All developing countries, including Southern Europe and certain Soviet bloc countries. Egypt, Indonesia, and India were often singled out. (Rated 7.4)

4. *Slow pay or increased defaults of export accounts.* Most South American and Southern European countries were listed:

also Mexico, India, Pakistan, Nigeria, and Poland. (Rated 7.4)

5. *Inadequate protection of copyright against large-scale piracy.* The principal offenders make a long list—Taiwan, Korea, China, Vietnam, Indonesia, Malaya, Singapore, Philippines, India, Pakistan, Nigeria, and several South American and Caribbean countries. Obviously this is a serious problem that can be remedied only by diplomatic action by the Department of State, backed up by the Department of Commerce and the federal office of the U.S. Trade Representative. Naturally, most publishers and book exporting firms think their interests have been neglected far too long by the responsible federal agencies. They feel that, failing correction by adherence to an international copyright convention, or by stronger police enforcement of the local copyright laws, our government officials should press for simple bilateral copyright treaties that will have force enough to command respect and full compliance. They point to the USSR's final capitulation, which came, seemingly, as a concomitant to the pursuit of improved trade relations with the United States. (Rated 6.5)

6. *High mark-up of U.S. list prices by many exporters, local importers, and booksellers.* This is a problem the world over—in industrialized as well as developing countries. As noted earlier, every successful importer *must* mark-up prices enough to cover the costs of his importing and investment expense, yet many foreign book buyers seem to feel that any mark-up at all is robbery by a greedy middleman. And often enough the rate of mark-up does border on robbery—of a customary and reasonable sort, to be sure. The crux of the matter, of course, is how much mark-up is justified in a given area. And here is where opposite interests and sympathies frequently clash shrilly. And double trouble frequently occurs when retail booksellers put a stiff mark-up on top of that of the importer. In some developing countries, the double marked-up price is 50 percent, or even 100 percent, above the U.S. list when the book appears on the retailer's shelf. But this seems not to disturb many booksellers who cater only to the "carriage trade." A few high-priced sales will enable them to keep shop only half the day. How can a U.S. exporter of the greatest wisdom and goodwill change the nature of an indifferent or indolent bookseller in Bangkok or Bolivia? (Rated 6.0)

7. *Failure to allocate sufficient public funds for purchase of books and other cultural materials.* This is a well-known endemic failure of all underdeveloped countries, and of some that are quite prosperous. (One of our respondents even listed the United States!) In many countries it appears to be a case not of "guns or

butter" but of "guns or education and culture." Clearly, it is a problem for which only local political solutions can be found. (Rated 5.4)

8. *Imposition of duty or other forms of impost on importation of books and similar products.* Several Latin American and Middle East countries, plus Australia, New Zealand, Indonesia, Egypt, Nigeria, and South Africa, appear to be the biggest offenders in contributing to what is, of course, a local deterrent. The importers must pay the duty, and this adds to the prices of—and increases buyer resistance to—most types of books. Many countries prohibit import duty on books by their adherence to the UNESCO treaty known as "The Florence Agreement," but some of them fudge this agreement by imposing an "added-value" tax or some other form of impost on landed goods. (Rated 4.8)

9. *The use in tertiary education of lecture notes "cribbed" from U.S. books.* This is a traditional practice in several areas of the world, notably Latin America, Southeast Asia, and the Middle East. In each it has substantially crimped the sale of printed texts and reference books. The notes usually are duplicated by the lectures and sold directly to their students, often at prices that are higher than those of available standard textbooks. And in many universities of developing countries, it is readily admitted that students who can afford to buy the lecture notes have a much better chance of receiving higher marks. Publishers cannot object to this teaching method because it is, of course, an inheritance from the classical method of European education. They can rightly object to the flouting of copyright protection, however, but this usually is not effective. In fact, many Third World educators depend on the sale of their lecture notes as a professional prerogative that provides a sustaining portion of their income. So, for this deterrent, most exporting publishers wisely "grin and bear it." (Rated 4.1)

10. *Taxation or other imposts on profits earned locally by U.S. exporters, or on the transfer (repatriation) of earned surpluses.* In a few countries, the rate of taxation of locally earned profits (or of the repatriation of earned surplus by externally owned minority interests) is so high as to discourage foreign investment in developmental projects. India is the chief offender in this respect; its taxation is 50 percent of operating profits. Other countries that have onerous rates of taxes on the export of profits are Mexico, Brazil, and Argentina. Naturally, the governments of these countries argue that they need the income, and that their tax reduces the amount of U.S. tax paid. Nonetheless, the psycho-

logical factor is powerfully negative in the minds of U.S. publishers. (Rated 3.8)

11. *Extralegal expense of undercover payments to custom officials, dock foremen, forwarding agents, et al., used to speed up import shipments.* Making such payments is customary, even necessary, in most Latin American countries, in many Asian countries, and in some African countries. Without these payments ("Backsheesh"), incoming shipments can lie on docks or in custom's warehouses for weeks on end. (Rated 3.5)

12. *Increased competition from English-language books from other countries, notably Great Britain, West Germany, Canada, France, and the Scandinavian countries.* Although such competitive books have increased rapidly over the past decade (as noted in Part 4), they have not yet become a major factor except at the advanced levels of scientific, technical, medical, and industrial treatises and monographs. But even here the increased competition has a special importance, because U.S. publishers of such books had come to count on exports for 50 percent or more of their total sales. Faced with further competitive losses of overseas sales, U.S. publishers (and authors) may see their production of such books sharply diminished in the future. (Rated 3.3)

13. *Increased competition from audiovisual materials and computer-based information and informational systems.* There is no such competition in any developing countries; and some, but of no great consequence, in Northern European countries. These modes as replacements of books appear to be causing publishers very little loss of sleep—as yet, anyhow. (Rated 2.6)

14. *Increased national disaffection or hostility to U.S. products.* Only Iran and a few Latin American countries were listed as places where this factor had any importance at all. (Rated 1.9)

Judging by the frequency of "specific mention" of countries or areas that are currently the more difficult for U.S. exporters, three general areas led by expected margins: South America (17 mentions); Sub-Saharan Africa (12 mentions); and North Africa (11 mentions). Countries singled out as offering current obstacles most frequently were: India (14 times), Nigeria (13), Pakistan (11), Indonesia (9), Mexico (8), and Egypt (7). At the lowest end, Poland and the Dominican Republic were each mentioned twice, and Chile once.

It would be unreasonable to expect that any of the foregoing fourteen deterrents will disappear in the near future. Rather, it appears that some of them will become more onerus until world economic conditions have improved and the widened gap between "have" and "have-not" nations has been somewhat reduced. Meanwhile, it is clear that both the U.S. book industry and certain U.S. government agencies should quicken their efforts toward improvements whenever and wherever opportunities present themselves.

PART 9

Whose Responsibility
Is It, Anyway?

Before discussing the question of responsibility for the welfare of
the U.S. book abroad, we should review some of the many basic
values and uses of the book in a civilized society—with special
reference to Third World countries. (This litany is very familiar, of
course, to book publishers and librarians; it will be obvious,
surely, to many other readers.)

To put it broadly, U.S. books serve developing countries in
several ways: they stimulate and guide the development of natural resources; they assist basically in the development of human
resources; they foster better understanding of our beliefs, faiths,
institutions, enterprises, and modes of living in our vastly hetero-
geneous society; they cultivate the intellect, the spirit, the crea-
tivity, and the innate yearning of every individual for freedom and
opportunity to improve his or her way of life and give it more
meaning.

To put it from the U.S. point of view (that is, narrowly and less
loftily), the export of our books has various values to several
discrete segments of our society:

—To authors, they are the products of their talent and hard-
won skill, of their gifted imagination and their special knowledge, even of their blood, sweat, and tears. Naturally, most
authors want the world to share the value of their inspired and
highly toilsome creations.

—To editors, publishers, and booksellers, they are products to
be perfected and manufactured, then sold as widely as possible. As explained earlier, overseas sales added to domestic
sales substantially reduce unit costs and prices of many kinds
of books. Indeed, without the prospect of sizable export sales,
many very valuable specialized books could not be published at
all.

—To businessmen, industrialists, and financiers, they condition
overseas markets and increase exports of U.S. products and
services. This is the manifestation of the classical trade-fol-

71

lows-the-book credo. Further, for most multinational corporations and traders, books serve as invaluable tools for indoctrination and training of the vast indigenous personnel required for overseas operations.

—To transportation companies, travel agencies, and international hotel operators, they serve as indispensable directories and guides on where to go, where to stay, what to see, and what to buy abroad. Thus books stimulate tourism and help to increase both domestic and foreign income and profits.

—To research scientists and professional practitioners, they are essential conduits for international exchanges of problems, methods, discoveries, and solutions. Here books serve universally to help break down even the strongest barriers to international cooperation and goodwill.

—To engineers, architects, and construction firms, they often are precursors to the winning of overseas contracts; and overseas contracts usually result in the specification and purchase of U.S. materials, machines, and operating equipment.

—To educators they help to qualify thousands of the better foreign students for graduate study and research in the United States.

Now, to the foregoing list of private-sector benefits, one can add several categories of governmental benefits that are derived, either directly or indirectly, from the sale and use of U.S. books in Third World countries:

—They smooth the path for the pursuit of our foreign policies. It has been said often that next to people, books are our best ambassadors of international enlightenment and goodwill. This is especially true of the U.S. textbooks and professional books that are studied abroad by university students and other young intellectuals. In most Third World countries, the revolutionaries of today are leaders of tomorrow, and the political power of young readers can be ignored by a government only at its own peril. Hence, in such countries U.S. books—and especially U.S. textbooks at university level—are directed to the hands of young men and women who are vital to both the future of their country and the future of relations between their country and ours. This is, to be sure, the thought that F.D.R. had in mind when he declared, "Books are bullets in the battle for men's minds."

—They serve importantly, as noted above, in the development of natural and human resources of all Third World countries.

Thus they will help, indirectly and eventually, to relieve our government of much of its perenially heavy burden of foreign economic assistance.

—They help in the same way to relieve the severe imbalances of trade with the United States and thus alleviate the paralyzing shortages of hard currency in most Third World countries.

—They are the best and most portable evidence of the cultural achievements of the United States. This is obvious, but the need abroad for more knowledge and better appreciation of American arts and letters is not as obvious as it should be to many U.S. citizens. Our political competitors and detractors strive constantly to build up an image of the United States as a nation of materialistic, money-mad, ruthless "Yankee Traders" who have little or no regard for the finer things of life. Books and more books are, of course, the best available antidote for this denigrating propaganda. Anyone who has traveled widely abroad knows that it would be a mistake to underestimate the critical nature of this particular international battlefield of ideology and political power.

A highly important general value of the exported U.S. book is neither so evident nor so tangible as those just described. This is its influence in maintaining English as the lingua franca of most of the world. It would be difficult to exaggerate the importance of having and keeping English as the international language of education, science, industry, and commerce, or to exaggerate the power of our books in keeping it so. Here again, there is far too little public appreciation of this fundamental, far-reaching value.

Finally, it should be noted that, in the end, a book costs less, lasts longer, and penetrates more deeply than any other means of international communication of information and ideas. In all Third World countries a book usually passes through the hands of ten or twenty readers, or even more. Indeed, certain kinds of books are handed down from generation to generation. The problem usually clearly comes with the ubiquitous first obstacle—the high price of the original purchase.

Yet, despite all the contrary evidence and arguments that have been cited over and over again, there still are many leaders in both our government and our private sector who are convinced that book exporting is no more than a commercial enterprise that should be able to look after its own particular problems. Naturally, book publishers and exporters look upon this view as being not only uninformed and short-sighted but actually against the best commercial, political, and humanitarian traditions of our country. They know that, try as hard as they may, they cannot possibly muster enough effort and resources of their own even to begin to fill the yawning book gaps that exist in all Third World nations of the world. They know, too, that several other industrialized countries, our rivals for trade and goodwill, are now overtaking our leadership in assisting developing countries to acquire the kinds and amounts of books that meet their minimal needs. Further, they know that thousands of other Americans with tangential interests share their view and their present sense of anxiety and frustration.

So it all seems to boil down to a matter of educating public opinion. Increased hundreds of opinion-makers and purse-string-holders must be shown that the U.S. book abroad is far more than an ordinary commercial commodity—that it is, in fact, in the vanguard of all our battles to improve our nation's present position and its future relations with all countries of the world. Then the conglomerate of true-believers must be organized nationally for effective action as promptly as possible. For it is truly a national responsibility and can be met only by a truly national response.

PART 10

The Future: A Suggested Plan

Now, what of the future—as far ahead as can be seen at the moment? What can be done to check the faltering role of the U.S. book in developing countries? And what of the "uncommitted" Third World countries in particular?

It seems quite certain that, for the present, the challenge will have to be met largely by private-sector initiative. Given the current restrictions on nonmilitary federal spending, it is obvious that new large-scale federal programs for overseas dissemination of informational, educational, and cultural materials cannot be expected in the immediate future.

So how can the private sector best mobilize interests and forces to fill a need that is becoming a national embarrassment? The best response, we believe, would be a coalition of the resources and competence of the many, many private individuals and organizations that have commercial or humanitarian interests in maintaining a strong American presence in the developing countries that need and welcome our aid. The organization of such a coalition would be, without doubt, a large task. But surely it would not be beyond accomplishment by a public-spirited band of informed and dedicated leaders. We believe that this kind of leadership can be mustered under the right kind of sponsorship.

Bolstered by the foregoing beliefs, we urge the creation of a nationwide initiative in the form of a not-for-profit organization under some such title as "National Coalition on Books for Developing Countries" or "U.S. International Book Council." Membership would be drawn by invitation to individuals, institutions, professional societies, trade associations, and corporations (public and private) that have demonstrable interests in the objectives of the organization (henceforth referred to simply as TO). Initially, an organizing committee of, say, twelve members would be formed. It should represent in equal proportions U.S. authors, publishers, government agencies, and nonbook commercial enterprises that have large multinational operations. This committee should be organized with the thought that it would become the central executive committee when the operating stage was reached. At that stage, TO would be formalized as a nonprofit, pro bono publico corporation, and thereafter it would function autonomously.

The organizing committee should also elect a board of directors of some eighteen to twenty members for terms of four years on a rotating basis. Thus the highly desired continuity of interest, knowledge, and leadership would be ensured.

TO would be structured into divisions, perhaps as many as twenty, each of which would represent a major kind or area of international interest, and each of which would be free to initiate and operate programs of its own with guidance and assistance from a centralized professional staff. The following groupings are suggested as examples of possible divisions:

1. Book publishers, booksellers, book exporters

2. Magazine and newspaper publishers

3. Broadcasting organizations and news agencies

4. Advertisers and advertising agencies

5. Retailing organizations

6. Manufacturers and manufacturing organizations

7. Extractive industries (oil, gas, chemicals)

8. Pharmaceutical manufacturers

9. Manufacturers of medical and hospital equipment

10. Mining, metals, and minerals

11. Food and food processing industries

12. Shipping and transportation

13. Travel agencies and associations

14. Hotels and hotel management chains

15. International sports organizations

16. International banking and finance

17. International accounting and auditing services

18. Educational associations and societies

19. Liquor and beverage producers and distributors

20. Ethnic, nationalist, and world-area promotional groups

21. Trade unions

22. Ecological and conservation groups

As to the permanent governance and management structure of TO, the following is suggested:

—Top government by a board of directors of twenty persons, all of whom have distinguished themselves and demonstrated interest in a discrete sector of TO's general area of activity. The members of the initial board would be appointed by the organizing committee and elected annually thereafter by the full membership.

—An executive director appointed as the top operating officer by the board.

—Two associate directors who would report to the executive director and would each have responsibility for one of the two groups of services described below.

—A business manager, who would also report to the executive director and be responsible for such functions as budgeting, accounting, payroll, personnel management, furnishing and equipment, and other operational details that customarily are handled by an office manager.

—All four operating officers would be supported by assistants and staff that would be employed as needed.

The two groups of services to be managed by the two associate directors are:

1. *Research, Planning, and Consultative Services.* This group would make contracted services available to government agencies, to TO's divisional members, and to any other foundation, institution, professional organization, corporation, or private individual that needs information and guidance in investigating or planning a noncommercial overseas book program. Also, it would provide consulting service for monitoring the operations of new services. For each instance of such contractual services, TO would bring together a team of experts recruited from its constituency or from private consultants. Further, this group would supply advisory service on specialized ancillary activities such as setting up seminars and workshops, organizing exhibits, preparing bibliographies and selective book lists, selecting effective testing and training materials, and organizing language-teaching programs, with emphasis on English as a second language. Here again, TO's function would be limited only to providing needed information

and guidance on available materials and outside professional competence.

2. *Program Management Services.* These services would be made available to the same clientele on a contractual basis for the management of new or ongoing projects or programs in TO's areas of interest. Here again, a competent management team would be recruited for each job, and each contracted job would be made self-supporting by including all its direct costs, plus a rate of overhead expense to cover related general and administrative services provided by TO. Similarly, TO would expand its staff and facilities only in pace with the growth in number and size of its contracted programs. Operating service functions would be subcontracted whenever possible to professional organizations or commercial firms.

TO's initial funding and continuing financial support should come from three sources: membership fees, private contributions, and income from contracted services. Appropriate annual membership fees (to be used for basic "institutional" support) might begin at $100 for individual members and $1,000 for institutional and corporate members. Foundations would be solicited for grants adequate to cover start-up expenses for the first two or three years.

Our very rough estimates place start-up and net operating costs at a maximum of $400,000 for the first year, $600,000 for the second year, $600,000 for the third year, and $200,000 each for the fourth and fifth years. Thereafter, all costs would be covered completely by contracted-services income and membership dues.

As to memberships and dues derived therefrom, it seems reasonable that, given proper sponsorship and an active organizing committee of prominent people, no fewer than 500 personal memberships and 100 corporate or institutional memberships could be enlisted in the first year, and these numbers should be doubled in the second year. If so, dues income would be $150,000 for the first year, and $300,000 for the second year. Thus, $450,000 of the $1 million start-up costs would be derived from dues income. If additional income of $50,000 could be realized from contracted projects in the two years, a balance of $500,000 in foundation or private grants would be needed. These are, to be sure, large figures, but they are, we believe, realistic requirements for mounting a significant private-sector initiative.

Further, it should be understood that the foregoing estimates of required expense funding do not represent projected operating budgets of TO. Rather, it would be expected that these funds together with overhead income from contracted services might amount to operating budgets as high as $5 million to $10 million for the fourth or fifth year. This would depend, of course, on the extent of the stimulated use of the service facilities, which in turn would depend largely on the state of the national economy.

Now, a few concluding summary remarks about TO as it has been conceptualized above:

—It should be organized by people who are convinced that its mission is a *national* responsibility, not a responsibility of either the government or the private sector alone. Without wide recognition of this fact, it is unlikely that we shall be able to check the diminishing distribution and influence of U.S. books abroad.

—It should function as closely as possible on the operating pattern of the British Council. This means that it should avoid political influence and socioeconomic bias. It should not undertake the management of any program that is basically designed for propaganda purposes, either overtly or covertly.

—Its divisional activities should follow the model set by Books for Asia. In fact, that organization could serve as an ideal for satellite divisional activities of TO.

—It should strive for stability and continuity in the management of both its central and divisional programs. This operating principle should apply especially to services performed for the government. And it should always be wary of factional political influences that often can obtrude in governmental programs.

—It should encourage programs that are designed to provide developing countries with the kind of books that they themselves want, not the kind that U.S. sponsors, either public or private, think they need.

—For top administrators and middle-management personnel, it should employ only seasoned professionals who have had overseas experience or demonstrated technical competence. It might well look first for such personnel among recently retired publishers, editors, librarians, career diplomats, and education specialists. The pool of competent and still vigorous retirees grows larger each year.

—It should work closely with the British Council and the Canada Council on common-interest objectives, and with the book-trade associations of the two countries. It should work also with the World Bank component units and with other intergovernmental agencies that share TO's interests and objectives.

—Since proper timing is all-important to TO's prospect for success, there should be no effort to make a formal start until the U.S. economy has improved substantially and until the present restrictions on nonmilitary federal spending have been further relaxed. For the successful start of a national venture of the size that we have recommended, the morale of both government budgeters and private-sector leaders needs to be considerably higher than it is at the moment. Yet the United States cannot afford to neglect its faltering position much longer. Decisions must soon be made on whether the cause will be won or lost.

Meanwhile, if the question of timing should be deemed too uncertain, it would be wise to form a smaller ad hoc committee for the purpose of organizing and funding a study of the feasibility of TO as a national initiative along the lines here proposed. This would not be a very large, or costly, or time-consuming research task, and it would be at least a tentative step in the right direction.

SOURCES OF
INFORMATION

A great deal of the information presented in this study was taken from sources that are not generally available to the public: the author's personal experience; notes on his interviews with others; unpublished memoranda and reports (private, corporate, institutional, governmental); and, in a few instances, confidential facts and figures that cannot be identified. Hence, the specificity of conventional footnotes or end notes has been avoided as these would be useless or equivocal in most instances. Some readers, however, may be interested in the following selected list of publicly available information sources that were consulted as the study progressed.

Altbach, Philip C. *Publishing in India: An Analysis*. Delhi: Oxford University Press, 1975.

Association of American Publishers. *Industry Statistics*. New York, 1974–81.

The Asia Foundation. *The President's Review: 1981 Annual Report*. San Francisco: Asia Foundation, 1982.

Barker, Ronald, ed. *The Book Trade in the USSR: Report of a Delegation of British Publishers, 1964*. London: The Publishers Association, 1964.

Barker, Ronald, and Robert Escarpit, eds. *The Book Hunger*. (Paris): UNESCO, 1973.

BCMA Associates, Inc. *Relationships among the National Institute of Education, Federally-Funded Educational Research and Development Agencies, and Commercial Publishers*. New York: BCMA Associates, 1977.

Benjamin, Curtis G. *International Publishing Becomes Multinational Publishing*. York, Pa.: The Maple Press Company, 1971.

Benjamin, Curtis G., ed. *Books for Developing Countries: A Guide for Enlisting Private-Industry Assistance*. New York: Franklin Book Programs, 1969.

Benjamin, Curtis G., and W. Bradford Wiley, eds. *Book Publishing in the USSR: Reports of the Delegations of U.S. Book Publishers 1962 and 1970*. Cambridge: Harvard University Press, 1971.

The British Council. *Annual Report 1981–1982*. London: Her Majesty's Stationery Office, 1982.

The Canada Council, Writing and Publishing Section. *Programs in Writing and Publishing*. Ottawa: The Canada Council, 1982.

Government of Canada, Department of Industry, Trade and Commerce. *Program for Export Market Development*. Ottawa, 1982.

Cole, John Y., ed. *The International Flow of Information: A Trans-Pacific Perspective*. Washington: Library of Congress, 1981.

Cole, John Y., ed. *U.S. International Book Programs 1981*. Washington: Library of Congress, 1982.

Dessauer, John P., ed. *Book Industry Trends 1982*. New York: Book Industry Study Group, Inc., 1982.

ESDUCK. *Goals and Achievements*. Cairo: The Egyptian Society for the Dissemination of Universal Culture and Knowledge, 1980.

International Publishers Association. *IPA Publishing News: Regulation of Book Imports*. No. 88. Geneva, 1981.

Krishnan, T.V.K., ed. *Book Development: Some Current Problems*. New Delhi: Dina N. Malhorta Publisher, 1969.

Lottman, Herbert R. "The Soviet Way of Publishing." *Publishers Weekly*, September 18, 1978.

Machill, Horst. *Buch und Buchhandel in Zahlem*. Frankfurt am Main: Buchhandler-Vereiningung, 1982.

The National Enquiry into Scholarly Communications. *Scholarly Publishing: The Report*. Baltimore: John Hopkins University Press, 1979.

Neumann, Peter H. *Publishing for Schools: Textbooks and the Less Developed Countries*. Washington: World Bank, 1980.

Neumann, Peter H., and Maureen A. Cunningham, eds. *Mexico's Free Textbooks: Nationalism and the Urgency to Educate*. Washington: World Bank, 1982.

Russak, Ben. *Scholarly Publishing in Western Europe and Great Britain*. The Annals of the American Academy of Political and Social Science, September 1975.

Smith, Datus C., Jr., *American Books in the Non-Western World: Some Moral Issues*. New York: New York Public Library, 1958.

Smith, Datus C., Jr. *The Economics of Book Publishing in Developing Countries*. Paris: UNESCO, 1977.

Sullivan, George, ed. *A Reason to Read: An International Symposium on the Promotion of the Reading Habit*. New York: UNESCO, 1976.

Tebbel, John. *A History of Book Publishing in the United States*. Vol. 4 (1940–1980). New York: R.R. Bowker, 1981.

United Nations Department of International Economic and Social Affairs. *World Economic Survey 1981-1982*. New York: United Nations, 1982.

UNESCO. *Statistical Yearbook 1981*. New York: Unipub, 1982.

U.S. Copyright Office. *Copyright Law of the United States of America*. Washington: Library of Congress, 1969.

U.S. Senate Committee on Appropriations. *Hearings on Public Law 480*. Washington: Government Printing Office, 1959, 1960, 1961, 1962, 1963.

U.S. Treasury Department, Bureau of Governmental Financial Operations. *Foreign Currencies Held by the U.S. Government 1981-1982*. Washington: Treasury Department, 1982.

APPENDIX A

USIA BOOK PROMOTION AND TRANSLATION PROGRAMS—1982

RATIONALE

Serious American books in English or in translation on themes of concern to USIA are essential to the agency's mission in public diplomacy. Books have unique qualities enabling them to provide foreigners substantive perceptions and insight into American society and government policies which they can get in no other way.

Today, such books face a major challenge abroad. Their distribution and readership have declined steadily in the Third World for many years while there is evidence that other nations, including the USSR, have increased significantly the distribution of their books and, thereby, their philosophies.

POLICY

The agency will promote significantly increased publication and distribution abroad of books in translation and in English which support or help explain our foreign policy, our institutions, and fundamental American values. These books are intended for use in USIA programs, in our libraries, at appropriate foreign institutions, and for sale to individuals interested in the United States.

A special effort will be made to identify and promote those books which are significantly relevant to current issues in international affairs and to immediate USIA policy and programming objectives. Various approaches will be used. They include a thorough survey of American books published by U.S. and foreign publishers and their acquisition for use in USIA programming; the promotion of titles selected by USIA for translation by foreign publishers (usually supported through guaranteed purchase of a certain number of copies for USIA); the direct publication by USIA of important titles unavailable from other sources; the assemblage of book exhibits on appropriate themes; and diligent efforts to encourage donations of relevant books from the American publishing industry for use with appropriate institutions and individuals abroad.

Agency policy also calls for increased cooperation with the American publishing industry in an effort to improve the general distribution of American books abroad, particularly those relevant to agency objectives.

APPENDIX B
THE UNITED NATIONS ROSTER OF "DEVELOPING" COUNTRIES

In a publication entitled *Towards a World Economy That Works* (1980), the United Nations classified 118 of its members as "developing" countries. It was explained that the classification was made "by broad descriptions, not definitions." In this context, it was further noted, ". . . 'developing' and 'developed' refer to the level of industrialization of countries and to a number of other indicators, including the level of Gross National Product, and the structural diversification of the economy." The subjoined official roster was produced under those guidelines. It is a melange that defies definitional use in the present study, but the number and the disparity of the nations included certainly are significant.

Afghanistan	Ethiopia
Algeria	Fiji
Angola	Gabon
Argentina	Gambia
Bahamas	Ghana
Bahrain	Grenada
Bangladesh	Guatemala
Barbados	Guinea
Benin	Guinea-Bissau
Bhutan	Guyana
Bolivia	Haiti
Botswana	Honduras
Brazil	India
Burma	Iraq
Burundi	Ivory Coast
Cape Verde	Jamaica
Central African Republic	Jordan
Chad	Kenya
Chile	Kuwait
Colombia	Lao People's Democratic Republic
Comoros	Lebanon
Congo	Lesotho
Costa Rica	Liberia
Cuba	Libyan Arab Jamahiriya
Cyprus	Madagascar
Democratic Kampuchea	Malawi
Democratic People's Republic of Korea	Malaysia
Democratic Yemen	Maldives
Djibouti	Mali
Dominica	Malta
Dominican Republic	Mauritania
Ecuador	Mauritius
Egypt	Mexico
El Salvador	Morocco
Equatorial Guinea	Mozambique

Nepal
Nicaragua
Niger
Nigeria
Oman
Pakistan
Panama
Papua New Guinea
Paraguay
Peru
Philippines
Qatar
Republic of Korea
Romania
Rwanda
Saint Lucia
Samoa
Sao Tome and Principe
Saudi Arabia
Senegal
Seychelles
Sierra Leone
Singapore

Solomon Islands
Somalia
Sri Lanka
Sudan
Suriname
Swaziland
Syrian Arab Republic
Thailand
Togo
Trinidad and Tobago
Tunisia
Uganda
United Arab Emirates
United Republic of Cameroon
United Republic of Tanzania
Upper Volta
Uruguay
Venezuela
Viet Nam
Yemen
Yugoslavia
Zaire
Zambia

APPENDIX C

EXPORT OF U.S. BOOKS BY TYPES
(Data extracted from BISG Annual "Trends")

Type of Book	Exports in $/millions		Percent of Type Exported		Percent of Type to Export Totals	
	1974	*1980*	*1974*	*1980*	*1974*	*1980*
Trade (Hardbound and Paperback)	34	59	6.0	4.8	11.9	11.6
Religious	6	13	4.3	4.1	2.2	2.5
Professional	93	178	19.5	17.7	31.8	34.9
Book Clubs	14	10	4.7	1.9	4.8	2.0
Mail Order	5	11	0.2	2.0	2.0	2.2
Mass Market Paperback	34	73	10.8	9.7	11.6	14.3
University Press	9	16	19.6	20.5	3.1	3.1
School (K-12)	20	24	3.2	2.5	6.8	4.7
College	56	99	11.9	10.3	19.3	19.4
Subscription— Reference	19	27	6.8	7.7	6.5	5.3
All Books	292	510			100.0	100.0

Note: The types of book follow the classification used in the statistical reports issued annually by the Association of American Publishers.

APPENDIX D

INFORMATIONAL MEDIA GUARANTEE PROGRAM
Inception to October 31, 1968

Countries	Program Began	Program Folded	Contracts Issued ($000 omitted)	Payments Made ($000 omitted)
Afghanistan	1961	1967	228	111
Austria	1949	1957	591	369
Burma	1958	1961	356	156
Chile	1955	1959	1,476	922
France	1951	1957	852	428
Germany	1949	1955	11,518	7,069
Guinea	1964	1967	80	32
Indonesia	1956	1963	7,738	6,163
Israel	1953	1961	15,406	12,099
Italy	1950	1951	83	9
Korea	1962	1968	2,081	1,051
Netherlands	1949	1954	2,866	1,839
Norway	1949	1957	586	315
Pakistan	1955	1967	4,139	3,023
Philippines	1953	1961	17,914	15,384
Poland	1953	1968	10,892	9,732
Spain	1957	1960	2,644	1,800
Taiwan	1953	1959	1,881	1,284
Turkey	1956	1962	8,951	6,829
Viet Nam	1956	1968	5,927	4,917
Yugoslavia	1952	1968	12,283	9,789
TOTALS for all countries			108,493	83,325

APPENDIX E

JOINT INDO-AMERICAN TEXTBOOK PROGRAM
Number of Editions and Copies Produced (1962–81)

Fiscal Year	No. Editions	No. Copies
1962	19	49,000
1963	34	88,900
1964	75	383,871
1965	146	493,300
1966	153	658,100
1967	154	595,600
1968	124	596,452
1969	212	879,173
1970	297	1,679,906
1971	78	329,330
1972	289	1,390,019
1973	48	220,744
1974	51	172,002
1975	125	382,811
1976	39	183,129
1977	18	67,500
1978	7	23,275
1979	5	16,750
1980	7	23,000
1981	4	10,500
TOTALS	1,885	8,243,362

Note: The sudden drop in production in FY 71 was due to the temporary curtailment of the P.L.-480 Textbook Program by the government of India at the time of the Pak-Indo War.

Three full-time American Book Program officers administered the program during its first ten years (FY 62-72); since FY 72 it has been under the general direction of the USIS librarian.

Some residual AID funds from the third "tranche" were utilized in FY 75, accounting for the sharp increase in textbooks published during that year.

APPENDIX F

USIA-SPONSORED BOOK
PUBLISHING PROGRAM, 1951–1980
(ooo copies omitted)

Fiscal Year	Translation Program	P.L. 480 Textbooks*	Published in U.S.	Total
1951	1,730	—	—	1,730
1952	3,310	—	—	3,310
1953	5,820	—	—	5,820
1954	4,360	—	—	4,360
1955	5,131	—	—	5,131
1956	5,987	—	633	6,621
**LPB 1956–60	4,346	—	—	4,346
1957	7,359	—	1,904	9,264
1958	6,814	—	873	7,687
1959	3,873	—	830	4,704
1960	4,746	—	659	5,406
1961	3,129	142	672	3,944
1962	3,545	476	1,082	5,104
1963	5,287	775	1,456	7,520
1964	8,317	1,078	1,776	10,801
1965	10,244	1,215	1,325	12,694
1966	8,855	789	1,599	11,243
1967	6,913	792	1,597	9,302
1968	4,999	696	835	6,530
1969	3,202	952	653	4,807
1970	2,593	1,761	517	4,873
1971	2,089	364	517	2,971
1972	2,029	1,436	655	4,121
1973	1,528	272	415	2,216
1974	1,256	229	620	2,105
1975	1,130	402	296	1,828
1976–5–Quarter	1,344	441	—	1,785
1977	881	106	—	987
1978	768	23	—	791
1979	565	16	—	581
1980	502	23	—	525
	123,664	11,994	18,923	154,491

*P.L. 480 Textbooks, primarily in English and in India, were financed by foreign currency generated from the sale of agricultural products.

**Low-Priced Book Programs produced for export sales through commercial firms.

APPENDIX G

THE ASIA FOUNDATION
Distribution of Books and Journals
by Countries (1954–1981)

Country	Total Volumes	Books	Journals
Afghanistan	100,692	87,832	12,860
Bangladesh	1,333,553	1,158,613	174,940
Burma	110,959	88,925	22,034
Cambodia	9,196	8,591	605
Hong Kong	120,500	104,762	15,738
India	670,434	499,833	170,601
Indonesia	824,331	628,291	196,040
Japan	2,516,260	2,195,901	320,359
Korea	938,198	721,320	216,878
Laos	18,290	15,883	2,407
Malaysia	1,220,998	1,185,166	35,832
Maldives, Republic of	5,901	5,901	0
Nepal	11,778	9,194	2,584
Pacific Islands	90,269	89,174	1,095
People's Republic of China	85,994	23,761	62,233
Pakistan	830,751	719,682	111,069
Philippines	7,945,397	7,315,028	630,369
Singapore	173,114	168,402	4,712
Sri Lanka	291,939	272,270	19,669
Taiwan	325,080	277,851	47,229
Thailand	295,465	231,960	63,505
Vietnam	842,830	809,758	33,072
GRAND TOTAL	18,761,929	16,618,098	1,143,831

APPENDIX H
THE AD HOC ADVISORY COMMITTEE

This study, commissioned by the Center for the Book, was prepared with help from many members of the center's national advisory board. Listed here are members of the ad hoc committee formed to serve as advisers for this project. Its members are from the advisory board of the Center for the Book, the Association of American Publishers, and the U.S. Information Agency.

Leo N. Albert, *Chairman*
Chairman of the Board, Prentice-Hall International, Inc.

Saundra L. Smith, *Secretary*
Director, International Division
Association of American Publishers, Inc.

Members

Robert E. Baensch
Vice President—Marketing,
McGraw-Hill International Book Co.

Pierre B. Balliett
Vice President, Houghton Mifflin Co.
Director, International Division,
Houghton Mifflin Co.

John L. Beauchamp
Director, International Department
Random House, Inc.

Simon Michael Bessie
Director, Harper & Row, Inc.

Alexander J. Burke, Jr.
President, McGraw-Hill International Book Co.

Nicholas G. Chantiles
Vice President, International
Times-Mirror Book Co., Inc.

Paul E. Feffer
President, Feffer & Simons, Inc.
Chairman, International Division
Association of American Publishers, Inc.

W. Gordon Graham
Chairman & CEO, Butterworth Publishers, Ltd.

Kenneth Thurston Hurst
Ex-President, Prentice-Hall International, Inc.

Dan Lacy
Senior Vice President, McGraw-Hill, Inc.

Donald E. McNeil
Chief, Book Programs Division
U.S. Information Agency

Andrew H. Neilly, Jr.
Chairman & CEO, John Wiley & Sons, Inc.

Peter H. Neumann
President, Peter Neumann Associates, Inc.

About the Author

Curtis G. Benjamin, a major force at McGraw-Hill and in the publishing world for more than fifty years, completed this volume shortly before his death in November 1983 at the age of eighty-two. An informed spokesman for the U.S. book-publishing industry, he was also an effective promoter of multinational publishing and American book-exporting programs. His energy, innovative ideas, and contribution to American publishing were recognized in 1975 when his colleagues established the Curtis G. Benjamin Award for Creative Publishing, which is sponsored by the Association of American Publishers.

In 1952 Curtis Benjamin was elected director of the American Book Publishers Council and of the American Textbook Publishers Institute, two organizations which merged in 1970 to form the Association of American Publishers. "Uncle Ben," as he was affectionately known throughout the community of the book, served as chairman of the Book Industry Joint Committee on Copyright, 1959–65, 1971–72, and was chairman of the U.S. Book Publishers' Delegation to the USSR for the State Department in 1962. He served on numerous other committees and commissions, among them the Government Advisory Committee on International Book and Library Programs (chairman, 1962–64), the Science Information Council of the National Science Foundation (1959–60, 1964–67), the Asian Book Development Seminars in New Delhi and Singapore (cochairman, 1969), and the Ditchley Foundation Conference of Anglo-American Book Publishers (1969).

In 1962 the McGraw-Hill Book Company, which under Curtis Benjamin's leadership had extended original publishing to fifteen countries, received the first "E" award for excellence in book export development. After his retirement in 1966, Curtis Benjamin continued to serve as an adviser for the book-publishing industry, especially in promoting the international interests of books. Ever eager to learn, he gathered firsthand information about book publishing and distribution through travel in fifty-four countries around the world throughout his long career.